bags bags bags

bags bags bags

Dorothy Wood

NH

NEW
HOLLAND

First published in 2006 by New Holland Publishers (UK) Ltd
London • Cape Town • Sydney • Auckland

Garfield House
86–88 Edgware Road
London W2 2EA
United Kingdom
www.newhollandpublishers.com

80 McKenzie Street
Cape Town 8001
South Africa

Level 1, Unit 4
14 Aquatic Drive
Frenchs Forest
NSW 2086
Australia

218 Lake Road
Northcote
Auckland
New Zealand

ISBN 1 84537 248 6

Senior Editor: Corinne Masciocchi
Designer: Sue Rose
Photographer: Shona Wood
Production: Hazel Kirkman
Editorial Direction: Rosemary Wilkinson

2 4 6 8 10 9 7 5 3 1

Reproduction by Modern Age Repro, Hong Kong
Printed and bound by Times Offset (M) Sdn Bhd, Malaysia

contents

introduction

U nlike our grandmothers, few of us are content with only one bag. We need bags in a variety of shapes and sizes to see us through the day – from tote bags for everyday use to smaller decorative bags for evening wear or special occasions. Bags are quite definitely designed on the adage 'form follows function' as the things we need to carry determine their size and shape - the corduroy work bag on page 60 is large enough to carry knitting needles and wool, with lots of pockets for paraphernalia, whereas the tiny red velvet evening bag on page 29 will only hold a purse and keys. The design also depends on our lifestyle – city dwellers need bags that are secure or mould closely to the body, such as the tweed handbag on page 76 or the long-handled tote on page 48.

All bags have a handle of some sort, and because the type of handle very much defines the style of the bag, it has influenced the way the bags are featured in this book. The chapters include bags with fabric handles, bar handles, 'd'-shape handles and ring handles. Handles are made from all sorts of materials, such as wood, bamboo and acrylic and you can find a range of styles in each. This makes it easy to alter the look of a bag: choose a bright acrylic handle rather than bamboo and the look goes from natural to contemporary.

Change the fabric from soft tweed to brightly coloured canvas or PVC and the transformation is complete.

There is a huge choice of shapes and styles, from handbags to holdalls, and all the designs can be individually tailored to your own colour scheme or taste to create a truly unique bag. This is made possible because each bag has its own pattern, either drawn out and ready to enlarge, or where the pieces are a regular shape made from precise measurements included in the instructions.

Although a background in dressmaking is useful, you do not need any special skills to make any of the bags featured in this book. Each project has clear step-by-step instructions and detailed photographs guide you from cutting out to making up. If you are a novice sewer, read through the technique section before beginning so that you are familiar with some of the basic skills and refer back to the detailed instructions where indicated in the text.

Making your own bags has lots of advantages – it is not only hugely satisfying and enjoyable but by choosing your own fabric, colours and embellishments you will make a truly unique bag and with so many different designs to choose from you'll be busy for some time!

materials and equipment

The type of equipment used for making bags is very similar to that needed for dressmaking and sewing soft furnishings. You only need a basic sewing machine, which has straight stitch, although a swing needle machine that has zigzag stitch can be useful. Remember to match the size of the sewing machine needle to the weight of the fabric, otherwise you will find it keeps breaking. Size 80/90 (14/16) is ideal. Read through this section to give you an overview of the kind of materials and equipment that are suitable for bag making.

fabrics

Bags can be made from a wide range of fabrics – anything from sheer organza to heavyweight furnishing fabrics can be used; it all depends on the style of the bag. When you buy fabrics for making a bag, your first instinct will probably be to head for the dressmaking department, but it is likely that you will find more suitable fabrics in the soft furnishings or curtain material department.

Most bags for everyday use require a fairly firm fabric so that the bag holds its shape in use and is strong enough to hold your possessions or shopping. Furnishing fabrics have that extra strength yet are still easy enough to stitch. One of the other advantages of furnishing fabrics is the huge choice available. Search through the rails of hanging samples in your local department store for gorgeous fabrics such as the polka dot fabric used on page 43 and the lovely cream jacquard fabric on page 84. The minimum order is usually one metre (one yard) but even so, you will have a fairly inexpensive, totally unique bag.

linings

Linings are the fabrics used on the inside of the bag. The lining covers any interfacings or ugly seams and gives the bag a professional finish. It is important to give the lining as much thought as the main fabric. Linings are generally lighter in weight than the main fabric but you should choose the type of fabric depending on the style of bag. An evening bag can have a luxurious silk, satin or taffeta lining, whereas an everyday tote bag needs a more hard-wearing fabric. Choose colours or patterns that complement the main fabric – this doesn't mean that the lining has to match – it can be a complete contrast for a really funky look.

interfacings

(from the top: fusible bonding web; sew-in Vilene; lightweight woven iron-on interfacing; ultra-soft iron-on interfacing; iron-on canvas interfacing; fusible soft furnishing interfacing)

Interfacings are an essential component of bag making. They are used between the bag fabric and the lining, and you should generally attach the interfacing to the main fabric. The most practical interfacings are iron-on rather than sew-in as they support the fabric completely. You can even use a lightweight iron-on interfacing to give a length of dress fabric enough body to make a bag.

Whichever fabric you choose, it is likely that you will need to use an interfacing to support the shape of the bag. There is a huge range available, from ultra-soft, lightweight interfacings, to soft furnishing interfacings designed for tiebacks and pelmets. The interfacing you use will depend on the choice of fabric and the style of bag you are making. The step-by-step instructions for each bag suggest a type of interfacing to use, but you should try out your particular fabric with the interfacing to check if it is suitable.

bag handles

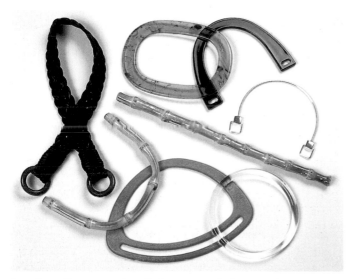

Bag handles come in all shapes and sizes and are available from craft or dress fabric shops. If you have difficulty finding them, refer to the suppliers' list to find a suitable mail order company or online store. All the handles used in this book are bought from the suppliers listed on page 95.

Bag handles are usually grouped according to the material they are made from and the most popular are acrylic, wood and bamboo. Clear acrylic handles, which come in a wide range of shapes, are particularly useful as they can be dyed to any colour using a hot-water dye (see page 17).

Once you have decided on a particular bag to make, look carefully at the style and size of handle. This is especially important if you are ordering from a catalogue or on the Internet. You can choose a handle made from a different material but try to find one that is the same size and shape.

bag findings

Findings is a group term for all the metal fitments or hardware used to make bags. Findings are readily available, and you can buy them at craft shops and

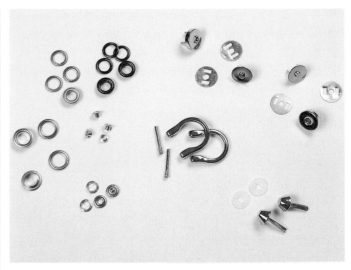

department stores. You can make bags without using these fitments but they do give a handmade bag that professional finish. Follow the manufacturer's instructions for fitting or follow the instructions in the project steps or techniques section.

Magnetic fastenings: these are specially designed as bag fastenings. There are two sections that fit through slits in the bag fabric and are secured on the reverse side. Choose from black, gold, brass or silver finishes.

Foot brads: these large studs protect the fabric on the base of the bag and are particularly useful if the bag has a stiff base. The brads are inserted through slits in the fabric and secured on the inside.

Bag handle loops: some U-shaped handles are attached with bag handle loops. The loops have a removable pin that slots through a hole in the handle.

Eyelets, snaps and poppers: these metal findings are usually sold with a fitting tool although you can buy special pliers. Snaps and poppers are used to secure or fasten, and eyelets to make neat holes in fabric. Small eyelets are ideal for straps or even to create decoration. Larger eyelets are used to carry the cord for duffle bags.

scissors

When cutting out, use a large pair of dressmaking shears. The longer blades give a cleaner cut, and remember to keep them just for fabric. Keep a separate pair of scissors for cutting paper as they will become too blunt to cut fabric. A small pair of sharp scissors, such as embroidery scissors, is useful for snipping and notching seams, and trimming threads.

techniques

The bags in this book all come with clear step-by-step instructions that are easy to follow if you have some dressmaking skills. If you are a novice stitcher, it will help to read through the techniques before beginning one of the bags and refer back for detailed instructions where indicated in the text.

enlarging patterns

Due to space restraint, it is not possible to include full-size patterns for the bag designs. The simplest way to enlarge the templates featured on pages 88–95 is by photocopying. Each template gives details of how much the pattern needs to be enlarged. Photocopy the template on to a sheet of A4 paper then enlarge on to A3 paper by the percentage indicated.

adding seam allowances

The patterns *do not* include seam allowances. The seam allowances to be added to the main fabric, lining and interfacing are 1.5 cm (5/8 in) unless otherwise indicated, although interfacings are usually trimmed as close as possible to the stitched seam to reduce bulk. You can add the seam allowances once the pattern has been enlarged if there is enough room on the paper or you can add them as you are cutting out. The technique is the same for both methods.

• Enlarge the template to the correct size. Using a tape measure or ruler, work around the edge of the pattern marking 1.5 cm (5/8 in) out from the edge. On straight sides you can space the marks out and join with a ruler, but on curved edges make the marks closer together for accurate cutting.

preparing the fabric

The way you fold the fabric ready for cutting out depends on the fabric you have chosen. Plain fabric poses no problems as it can simply be folded right sides together so that the selvedges) are together. Always fold fabric along the straight grain, i.e. along a thread of the fabric so that when the pattern pieces are cut they are straight.

• If the fabric has a bold pattern, such as that used for the embellished bag on page 52, or a large detail like this embroidered flower, cut the fabric in single layers to ensure the pattern is exactly where you want it.

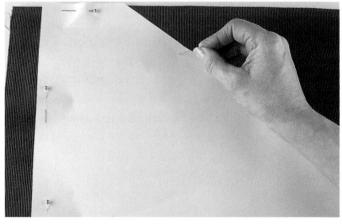

• Nap and pile fabrics, such as velvet and corduroy, can be folded in one direction only – with the pile or nap running in the same way as the fold. If you fold the other way, one side of the bag will have the pile going down and it will be going up on the other side. In general, the pile should be going up on the bag so that the fabric has a greater depth of colour.

cutting out

Fold the fabric as required and lay the pattern pieces out. Think about how the bag will look once the pattern pieces are cut out and made up as this may influence how you position the pieces. Gussets are particularly awkward and each fabric is different. A general rule is to concentrate on the main bag panels or the bit of the pattern piece that will be visible on the finished bag and match these sections.

• Pin the pattern with the straight grain line going across or down the fabric. Mark the seam allowances and cut out using large dressmaking shears for a smooth line.

marking the pattern pieces

Some templates have dots that need to be transferred to the fabric. The dots mark points on different pattern pieces that have to be matched, or where you need to stitch on seams. You can simply mark the fabric in the seam allowance with a pencil but it is better to work a tailor tack at each dot. To aid accurate pinning and stitching, you can also mark the position of sharp points such as the end of gussets with a tailor tack.

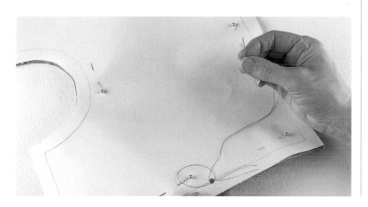

• Use a double length of brightly coloured thread, take a small stitch at the dot and leave a 2.5-cm (1-in) tail. Work a second stitch over the first and leave a large loop.

• Cut a 2.5-cm (1-in) tail at the other side. Pull the fabric layers apart and snip in between, leaving some thread strands on each piece.

stay stitching

Stay stitching prevents fabric from stretching while it is being made up. It is simply a row of machine stitching, worked on a single layer of fabric, usually around a curve.

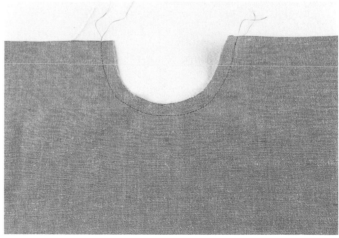

• Stitch with a normal machine stitch slightly inside the seam allowance so that the stay stitching will not be visible once the seam is stitched.

tacking

Tacking is a quick stitch that is used to hold two layers of fabric together while machine stitching. Begin with a knot and use a contrast colour so that the thread can be easily removed after stitching. Tacking is particularly important if you are matching a pattern or getting ready to stitch gathers.

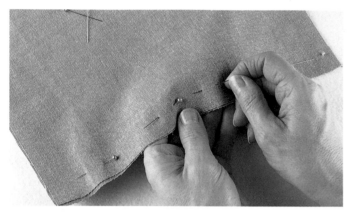

• Take a short stitch through the fabric then leave a larger gap before working the next stitch.

quick stitching without tacking

Fabrics used for bag making are often quite firm or have been backed with interfacing and so are quite easy to stitch without tacking.

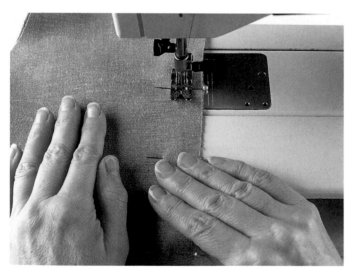

• Pin the layers together so that the pins go across the seam with the head of the pin sticking out over the raw edge. You can stitch over the pins and remove them as you go.

machine stitching

You do not need a fancy sewing machine to make bags, as the main stitch you will use is straight stitch with some zigzag stitch. Use a good quality sewing thread for bag making so that the seams are strong. Set the stitch length between 2 and 3. Use a machine needle to suit the weight of the fabric – a size 80 or 90 is ideal. Every time you change fabrics, check the stitching on a double layer of fabric and alter the top tension if required. The stitching should look the same on both sides with a tiny thread dot between each stitch.

top tension too tight

top tension too loose

correct tension

If the thread is lying across the top of the fabric, the top tension is too tight – move the tension dial to a lower number. If it is lying across the reverse side of the fabric, the top tension is too loose – move the tension dial to a higher number.

When stitching has the correct tension, the stitches on both sides of the fabric look the same. There should be a tiny dot between each straight stitch on both sides.

reverse stitching

Reverse stitching is used to secure threads at the end of a row of machine stitching or to strengthen a particular section of the seam.

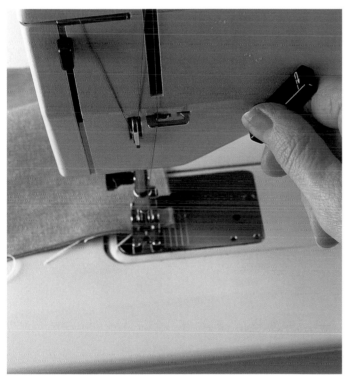

• At the beginning or end of a seam, simply switch the machine to reverse and go back over the previous stitching for about 2 cm (³/4 in).

gathering

Some of the designs in this book use gathering as a means of shaping the bag. Gathering can be worked by hand with two rows of small running stitches worked either side of the seam line but it is easier to gather by machine.

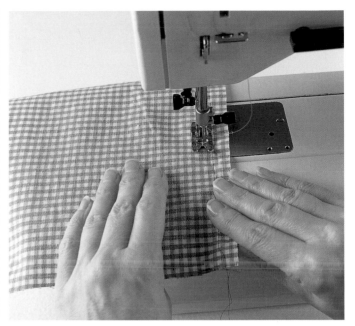

• Increase the stitch length to 4. Thread the machine with a contrasting thread colour. Stitch one row of gathering 0.3 cm (¹/8 in) on either side of the seam line. Use the lines on the footplate under the presser foot as a guide.

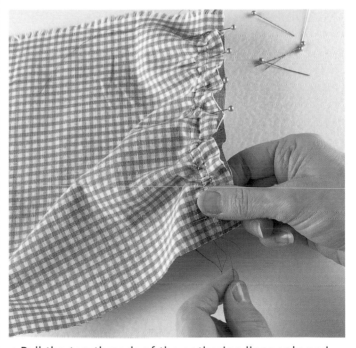

• Pull the top threads of the gathering lines only and ease the fabric along the threads until it is the length required. Insert a pin at either end and wrap the thread around to secure.

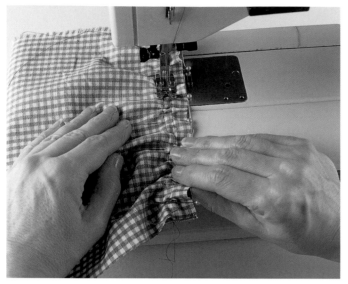

• You can stitch over pins but you will get a more even result if you tack the gathering in place and remove the pins before machine stitching. Change the stitch length back to 2–3 and machine stitch between the gathering lines. Pull out the gathering threads.

trimming

Seam allowances on all patterns are 1.5 cm (⅝ in) and once stitched, the seams can usually just be pressed flat. In some cases, however, you will need to reduce the size of the seam allowance to reduce bulk or to allow the seam to go around a curve neatly. Follow instructions in each project.

• Trim seams to 6 mm (¼ in). If the fabric is quite bulky and there are several layers, you can grade the seam allowance. Begin with the top layer at 3 mm (⅛ in) and trim subsequent layers slightly wider.

notching and snipping curves

Several of the bags feature curved lines as part of their design and require careful treatment for best results. Seams that are curved will not lie flat when turned through, unless the seam allowance is trimmed and then either notched or snipped.

• Trim curved seams to 6 mm (¼ in) and then notch concave (inward-facing) curves and snip into convex (outward-facing) curves.

pressing

Pressing or ironing is one of the most important techniques used in bag making and helps to produce a professional result. It is essential to press open seams at every stage.

• Pressing seams open reduces the bulk of the seam and allows layers of fabric to lie flat. For best results, you should 'set' the stitches by pressing along the stitching before pressing open.

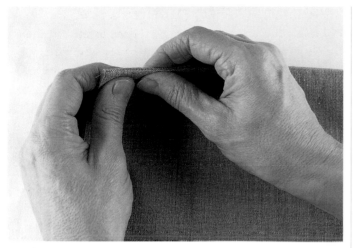

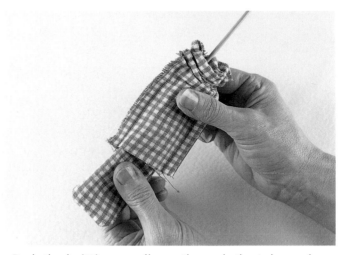

• When seams are positioned on the edge of a bag, press open the seam first if possible. Roll the fabric between finger and thumb to get the seam exactly on the edge before pressing.

turning rouleaux

Rouleaux are simply tubes of fabric, usually quite narrow, that can be used in place of cord for decorative features. The technique for turning rouleaux applies to tubes of varying width. Cut, fold and stitch the fabric strip as described in the step instructions. You can buy a tool called a rouleaux turner, but a knitting needle is just as effective.

• Push the knitting needle up through the tube and, at the same time, ease the fabric tube down over the needle. It is awkward to begin but gets easier.

top stitching

Although top stitching is considered a decorative element, it has a practical purpose, especially when used around the top edge of a bag or strap. The top stitching holds the seam exactly on the edge.

• Stitch across one end of the tube and trim the corners. Tuck one corner into the tube and insert the knob end of the knitting needle then pull the fabric gently over the knitting needle.

• Roll and press the seam as described above. Machine stitch close to the edge. To keep the stitching straight, use the edge of the presser foot as a guide and move the needle to the right if necessary.

stitches

Slipstitch is a useful stitch that should be almost invisible. There are two ways to work the stitch that both produce a similar result. Slipstitch is used to close a gap in a seam or to join two pieces of fabric neatly where strength is not required, for instance when fitting a lining.

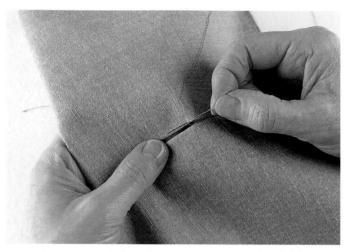

• To close a gap, bring the needle out on the fold at one side of the seam. Insert the needle exactly opposite on the other folded edge. Take a small stitch along the fold and then repeat the process in the other direction.

• To join two pieces of fabric invisibly, bring the needle out at the edge of the lining and take a tiny stitch on the main fabric. This stitch can be into the machine stitching. Take the needle back into the lining directly opposite and take a small stitch along the fold. Repeat to the end of the seam.

hemming

Hemming is a strong stitch used to secure two pieces of fabric. Even if the stitches are worked neatly, hemming is not invisible and is used where it will be hidden.

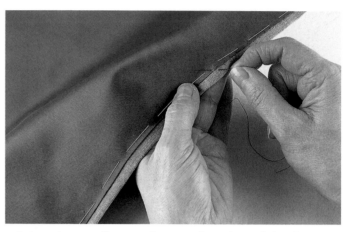

• Bring the needle out close to the edge of the front fabric. Insert the needle on the back fabric slightly further forward and take a diagonal stitch through to the front fabric again. Repeat to the end of the seam.

dyeing a cotton bag

Ready-made bags do not need to be pre-washed and can be dyed easily with cold-water dyes. The depth of colour you achieve will depend on the weight of fabric in the dye bath. Each tin will dye up to 225 g (8 oz) of fabric and so you can reduce the amount of dye accordingly. Once you have dyed your bag, buy gems, buttons or other embellishments to match rather than the other way round.

• Half fill a bucket with cold water. Dissolve the salt and a sachet of cold dye fix in hot water and add to the water in the bucket. Dissolve the dye in a pint of hot water and add to the bucket. Stir thoroughly with a large metal or plastic spoon.

• Soak the bag in warm water until it is completely wet and then add to the dye bath. Stir continuously for 15 minutes and then occasionally for the next 30 to 45 minutes.

• Wearing a pair of rubber gloves, lift the bag out of the dye bath and rinse in hot water with a tiny drop of detergent. Rinse in cold water until the water runs clear. Hang until almost dry and iron while still damp.

dyeing handles

Clear acrylic handles can be dyed any colour using hot-water dyes. You do not need any special equipment, but you may want to wear rubber gloves as the dye stains. Make sure you use a hot-water dye such as Dylon Multipurpose dye – cold water dyes will not work.

• Weigh 30 g (1 oz) of salt. Dissolve the Dylon dye in a pint of boiling water. Dissolve the salt and cold-water dye fix in another pint of hot water. Pour enough water into a large pot to cover the handles. Add the dye solution with the salt and the cold fix solution, and bring to a gentle boil. Drop the handles into the dye bath and keep them moving gently.

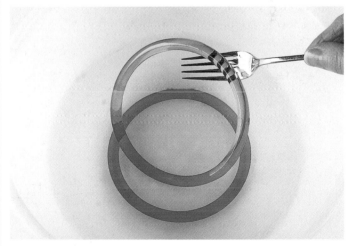

• Keeping the water at simmering point, turn the handles over after five minutes and keep moving for a further five. Lift the handles out using a fork or tongs and rinse them thoroughly in cold water.

projects

mini tote bag

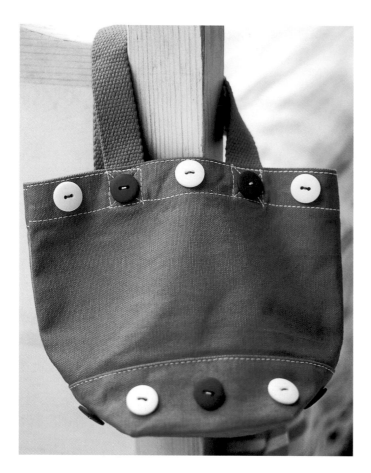

Give plain bags a personal touch with simple embellishments such as buttons, brooches or fabric motifs. You can buy ready-made bags in plain fabrics such as denim or various types of cotton fabric in white or cream.

materials

- Ready-made tote bag
- Tin of cold-water Dylon dye
- Sachet of cold dye fix
- 110 g (4 oz) household salt
- 10 white buttons
- 10 blue buttons
- Cotton sewing thread in white and blue
- Sewing needle

Dye the ready-made bag to the colour of your choice (see page 16) and for best results, press the bag while it is still damp. Choose buttons to tone in with the dyed bag and arrange on the bag until you are happy with the design. Sew on the buttons using a contrast thread and, for a neat finish around the top edge, try to stitch through the top layer of fabric only so that there is no unsightly stitching on the inside.

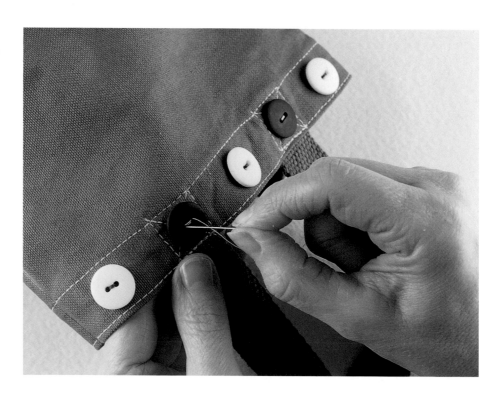

holdall

Fabric paints are a quick way to decorate a simple dyed bag. There are lots of different types of paint such as gloss, pearl and metallic that can be painted, stamped or applied using a nozzle, as shown here.

materials

- Ready-made holdall
- Tin of cold-water Dylon dye
- Sachet of cold dye fix
- 110 g (4 oz) household salt
- Cabochons in red, yellow, green and orange
- Fabric glue
- 3-D fabric paints in pink, yellow, green and orange
- 0.5-mm (No. 5) gutta nib

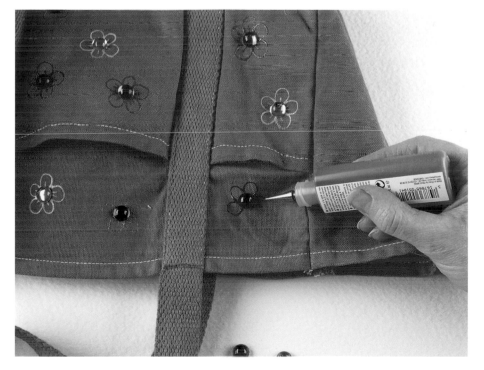

Dye the ready-made bag the colour of your choice (see page 16) and for best results, press the bag while it is still damp. Randomly arrange the cabochons over the bag avoiding two of the same colour together. Stick the cabochons in place with a dot of fabric glue. Attach the gutta nib to the bottle of 3-D paint and draw the petals in a matching colour. Decorate the petals with one or two short lines. Complete the design using the other paint colours. Leave the bag to dry flat for about 12 hours.

beaded shopper

Dye techniques such as tie-dye and batik can produce gorgeous patterns on simple cotton bags that can then be further embellished with embroidery and beads. The product used for this bag is called Easy Batik – it has a similar effect to hot wax but is much easier to use. You can draw out any motif on the bag – use giant punches such as this swirl for inspiration.

materials

- Ready-made shopper
- Pale pink and deep pink cold-water dyes
- Two sachets of cold dye fix
- 220 g (8 oz) household salt
- Giant spiral punch and sheet of paper
- Pencil
- Dylon Easy Batik
- 0.5-mm (No. 5) gutta nib and bottle
- Stranded embroidery cotton in deep red, fuchsia, orange and pale orange
- Approximately 25 ceramic washer beads

1 You can begin with a white bag, but for a more subtle effect, dye the bag pale pink (see page 16). When the bag is dry, insert a piece of card inside the bag to separate the layers. Punch or cut out your choice of motif several times and arrange on the bag. Draw around the motifs lightly with a pencil.

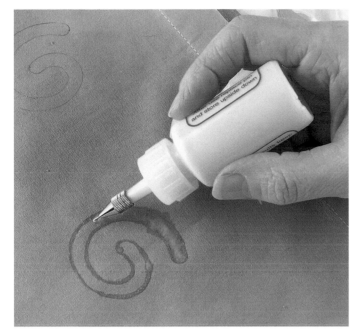

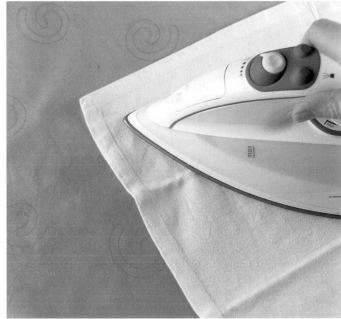

2 You can paint the Easy Batik or transfer to a gutta bottle for greater control. Shake the bottle well before use and make sure the Easy Batik penetrates the fabric. Go along the lines and then fill in.

3 Leave to dry for several hours then cover with a cloth and iron each area for 2 minutes.

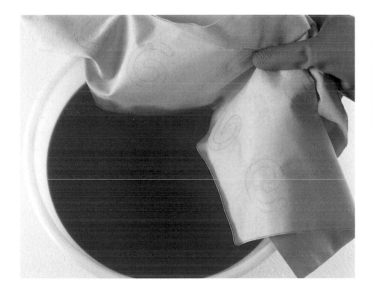

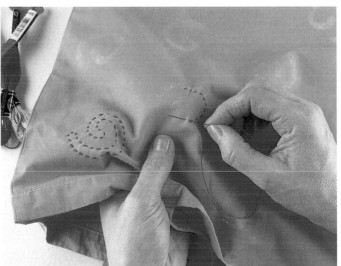

4 Now make a deep pink dye bath in a large container. Wearing rubber gloves, lower the bag into the dye and move about gently from time to time for up to 30 minutes. Lift the bag out and rinse in cold water until the dye runs clear. Wash in hot water with detergent to remove the Easy Batik.

5 Use simple embroidery to embellish the motifs. Two strands of cotton and running stitch along the pencil lines are very effective. You can vary the colours from motif to motif for a more colourful look. To complete the bag, attach beads in between the motifs with a few stitches.

dolly bag

A dolly, or Dorothy, bag is a traditional style that was originally used by bridesmaids to carry confetti, flower petals or rice for throwing over the happy couple. Made in white or cream silk with matching pearls, this dolly bag is the ideal accessory for any bride. Pearls can also be dyed in a wide range of pastel shades to match the bridesmaids' dresses, or choose pale grey and silver beads to make a beautiful pearl-encrusted and embroidered evening bag.

materials

- 45-cm (18-in) square of silver silk dupion
- 45-cm (18-in) square of ultra soft iron-on interfacing
- Pencil
- Silver embroidery thread and a needle
- Fifty 3-mm (⅛-in) round pearl beads in both silver and grey
- Seventy five 6-mm (¼-in) oat pearl beads in both silver and grey
- Small embroidery scissors
- 50 cm (20 in) fine silver cord or ribbon, for the tie
- 40 cm (16 in) medium silver cord, for the handle
- 45-cm (18-in) square of silver organza, for the lining

Seam allowances are 1.5 cm (⅝ in) and machine stitch is straight stitch.

1 Cut a piece of silver silk dupion 32 x 25 cm (12½ in x 10 in). Cut two pieces of interfacing, one measuring 32 x 15 cm (12½ x 6 in) and the other 32 x 9 cm (12½ x 3½ in). With all bottom edges aligning, place the larger piece of interfacing onto the silk then place the smaller piece onto the larger one, as shown in the picture. Iron in place. To position the bead motifs evenly but in a random pattern, mark pencil dots on the interfacing, leaving 3–4 cm (1¼–1½ in) between each dot and keeping the seam allowances clear.

2 Using a double strand of silver embroidery thread, bring the thread out at the first dot, pick up a round silver pearl and take the needle back through. Bring the needle up next to the pearl, pick up a grey oat pearl, and take the needle back through at the end of the bead. Sew another four grey oat pearls to create a flower shape. Work 6-mm (¼-in) straight stitches out from the centre pearl between each 'petal'. Alternating the colours of the pearls, work a bead flower on each dot.

3 In a space between the pearl flowers, sew a single round silver pearl. Work six lazy daisy stitches around the pearl (see diagram opposite) with two strands of silver embroidery thread to make small embroidered flowers. Work these embroidered flowers between the gaps of all pearl flowers, alternating the colours of the central pearl. Finally, fill in any gaps in the embroidered fabric with single round grey or silver pearls. Add some single pearls above the halfway point in a random fashion to soften the edge of the beading.

lazy daisy stitch

Bring the needle up through the fabric at A, make a loop and hold it with your thumb. Insert the needle back down through the fabric at A and up at B.

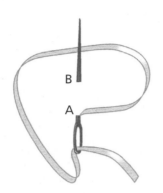

Make a small anchor stitch at B to hold the loop in place.

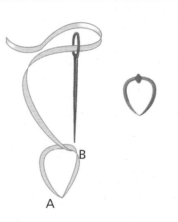

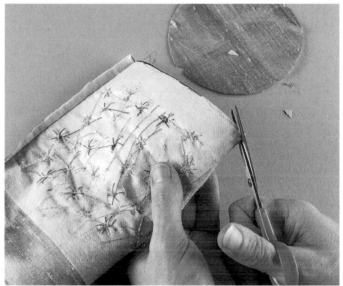

4 Iron a 3-cm (1¼-in) square of interfacing on the reverse side in the centre of the panel, 8 cm (3 in) from the top edge to reinforce the fabric before making the buttonholes. On the right side, in the centre of the square of interfacing, mark the position of two 7-mm (³/8-in) horizontal buttonholes with tacking thread. Using the buttonhole facility on your sewing machine, work the two buttonholes. Cut between the rows of satin stitch with small embroidery scissors to make the buttonhole openings. Now fit a zipper foot to the machine so that you can stitch beside the beads. Fold the silk bag panel in half widthways with the beads on the inside and stitch the back seam. Press open the seam.

5 To make the base, iron two 12-cm (4³/4-in) squares of interfacing one on top of the other on to the reverse side of a 12-cm (4³/4-in) square of silver silk dupion. Draw an 11-cm (4¼-in) circle on the interfacing and cut it out. Mark the circle into quarters with small notches on the outer edge, as shown in the photograph. Now fold the beaded bag panel into quarters and mark the bottom edge with notches in the same way as the circular base. Pin the circle into the base so that the notches match up and tack. Snip into the seam allowance of the bottom edge of the beaded bag panel to allow the fabric to lie flatter on the circle and then machine stitch. Trim the seam to 6 mm (¼ in).

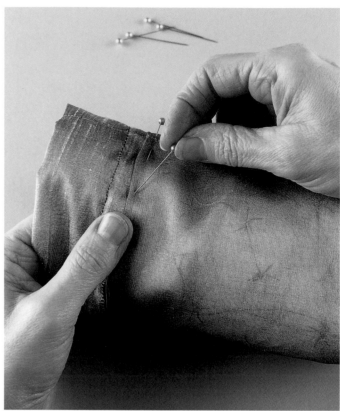

6 Fold over 5 cm (2 in) around the top of the bag. Machine stitch two casing lines 7 mm (3/8 in) apart either side of the buttonholes. Thread the fine silver cord or ribbon through the casing to make the tie. Now stitch the ends of the medium silver cord either side of the bag on the inside to make the handle.

7 To make a silk organza lining, cut a 32 x 17-cm (12 1/2 x 6 3/4-in) panel and an 11-cm (4 1/4-in) circle for the base. Stitch the back seam and inset the circular base in the same way as before (see Step 5). Turn the bag inside out, fold over the top edge of lining and tuck the bag inside. Slip stitch the lining to the casing stitching and turn the bag through.

tip

use one of the new ultra-soft iron-on interfacings to interface the silk as they give a softer effect than traditional interfacings.

velvet evening bag

Crushed velour has a gorgeous, opulent quality that is ideal for making an evening bag and because it is for the evening, it is worth going over the top with the embellishments. Ostrich feather trim and beautiful bead fringing are added to make this a really stunning bag. The bright red is ideal for teaming with that little black dress, but of course you can make the bag in any colour. Keep the feather trim, beads and crushed velour the same shade for a classic look.

materials

- 60 x 25 cm (24 x 10 in) red crushed velour
- 60 x 20 cm (24 x 8 in) ultra-soft iron-on interfacing
- Red sewing thread
- 20 cm (16 in) ostrich feather trim
- Red quilting thread
- Beading needle
- Beads: 2 tubes of size 11 red seed beads
    - 1 tube of 6-mm red flat oval beads
    - 1 tube of 6-mm red rice beads
    - 1 tube of 4-mm red faceted beads
    - 1 tube of 3-mm red teardrop beads
- 60 x 20 cm (24 x 8 in) red taffeta, for the lining

Seam allowances are 1.5 cm (⅝ in) and machine stitch is straight stitch.

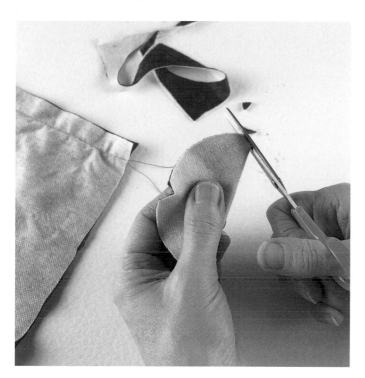

1 Iron two layers of interfacing on the reverse side of a 10-cm (4-in) square of red velour (if you have a heavier weight interfacing, one layer will be sufficient). Draw an 8-cm (3¹/₈-in) circle on the interfacing side and cut out. Now cut a 50 x 20-cm (19³/₄ x 8-in) piece of velour and iron one layer of interfacing the same size as the velour to the reverse side. Fold in half widthways with right sides together and machine stitch the back seam. Mark the circle into quarters with small notches on the outer edge and mark the tubular bag panel around the bottom edge in quarters in the same way.

2 Machine two rows of gathering stitches around the top and bottom edges of the velour tube (see Techniques, page 13). To do this, increase the stitch size to 4 and machine stitch 12 mm (¹/₂ in) in from the top edge and then 17 mm (³/₄ in) in from the top edge. Repeat with the bottom edge. Pull up the gathers around the bottom edge slightly and then, matching the notches, pin the circular base in place to the bottom edge of the tube. Adjust the gathers so that they are evenly spaced and tie off. Snip into the bottom seam allowance of the bag panel to flatten the fabric then machine stitch around the edge of the circle, removing the pins as you go. Pull out the gathering threads and then zigzag the seam and trim neatly.

tip

choose one of the new ultra-soft iron-on interfacings that will stretch slightly with the velour but give it enough body so that the bag holds its shape.

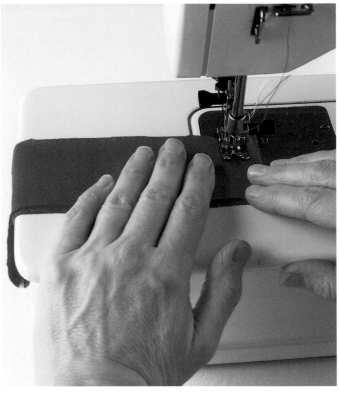

3 Turn the bag through and pull up the top rows of gathering stitches until the flattened bag measures 20 cm (8 in) across. Cut sections from the ostrich feather trim with about five or six feather fronds and tack in little groups around the whole top edge of the bag. Machine stitch across the feathers, just above the seam line. Triple zigzag across the ends of the feather trim to secure.

4 To make the binding, cut a 5 x 43-cm (2 x 17¹/₄-in) strip of velour. Fold it in half widthways so that right sides are facing. Machine stitch 2 cm (³/₄ in) into the back seam and reverse stitch out to the edge again. Repeat from the other edge to create the hole through which the gathering ribbon will be threaded. Press the seam open and set aside.

tip

ostrich feather trim often has a fabric binding that you should remove before snipping the trim into sections.

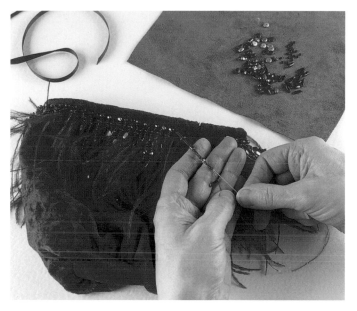

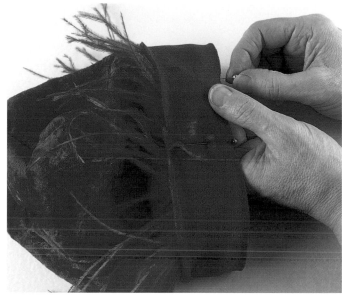

5 Thread a needle with a double length of red quilting thread. Bring the needle out below the binding on the right side. Pick up three seed beads and a flat oval bead, three seed beads and a rice bead, three seed beads and a faceted bead, three seed beads and a teardrop. Miss the last bead by taking the needle through the next bead and back up the bead strand. Sew a faceted bead at the top of the strand. Continue round the bag adding beaded fringe strands every 7 mm (3/8 in) just below the binding. Alter the number of seed beads or double the strand length occasionally.

6 With right sides facing and matching the back seam, pin the velour strip from Step 4 around the top of the bag. Machine stitch and then trim the seam to 1 cm (1/2 in). Fold the strip over the top edge of the bag and pin. Machine stitch around the bag just below the binding from the right side.

7 To make the strap, cut two 2-m (2-yd) lengths of red quilting thread. Thread both lengths through the needle and knot the ends together 15 cm (6 in) from the end. Pick up seven seed beads and then a decorative bead of your choice. Repeat until the strap is 50 cm (20 in) long and knot both threads together. Sew the ends of the strap into the bag on either side securely. Make a lining from a 20 x 43-cm (8 x 17-in) piece of red taffeta and an 8-cm (3 1/4-in) circle. Press under a 1.5-cm (5/8-in) turning around the top edge and tuck the lining in the bag. Pin and then hem to the machine stitching inside the top of the bag. Thread a length of ribbon through the casing and tie the ends.

duffle bag

Duffle bags are ideal when you are using public transport as you can have your hands free to hold on! They are also great if you have things to carry and need to hold on to young children or push a pram. This bag has been cleverly designed with a lining that has in-built pockets so that you can keep keys, mobile phones and other paraphernalia safe. The bag should support its own weight but use interfacing to add body to a lightweight fabric.

materials

- 1 m (1 yd) of 152-cm (60-in) wide spot fabric
- 50 cm (½ yd) of 152-cm (60-in) wide stripe fabric
- 50 cm (½ yd) iron-on medium-weight interfacing, optional
- 2.5 m (2½ yd) blue cord
- Eight 11-mm (½-in) silver eyelets and setting tool

Seam allowances are 1.5 cm (⅝ in) and machine stitch is straight stitch.

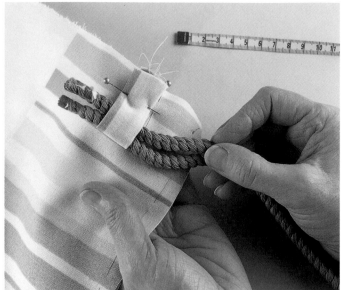

1 Cut a 73 x 42-cm (29 x 16$\frac{1}{2}$-in) piece of spot fabric and, if it is too soft, back it with iron-on interfacing. Cut a 73 x 15 cm (29 x 6 in) piece of stripe fabric so that the stripes are vertical along the length. Pin the stripe fabric to the spot fabric with right sides facing, 12.5 cm (5 in) from the bottom edge of the spot fabric. Machine stitch a 1.5-cm (5/8-in) seam, fold down and press. Tack the bottom edge.

2 Cut two 6.5 x 10-cm (2$\frac{1}{2}$ x 4-in) strips of stripe fabric, fold each in half lengthways and machine stitch 6 mm (1/4 in) from the cut edge. Turn the strips through and press. To make the bottom cord loop, fold one strip in half widthways and pin 4.5 cm (1$\frac{3}{4}$ in) from the bottom edge. Check that two thicknesses of cord will fit through the loop. Pin the back seam of the bag and machine stitch. To make the toggle, fold the second strip in half widthways and stitch a back seam. Turn through and open out the seam. Flatten so that the seam is in the centre and stitch down the seam line.

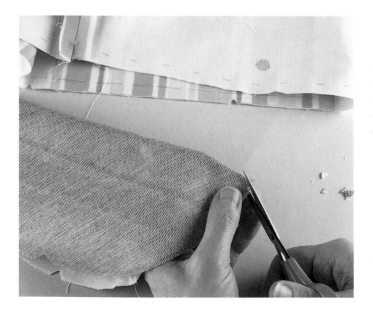

tip

if using a fabric with a one-way pattern, pin it upside down in Step 1 so that if ends up the right way up.

3 Cut a 25-cm (10-in) circle in stripe fabric and interface. Mark the circle in quarters with small notches on the outer edge. Mark the bottom edge of the bag in quarters in the same way and then pin the base into the bag, matching the notches. Tack the base then machine stitch. Trim the seam to 6 mm (1/4 in) and overlock or zigzag.

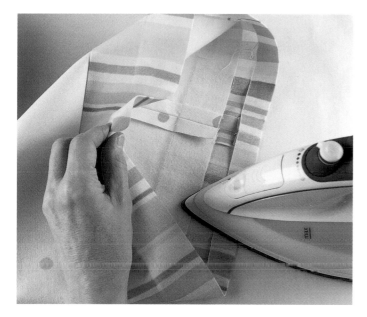

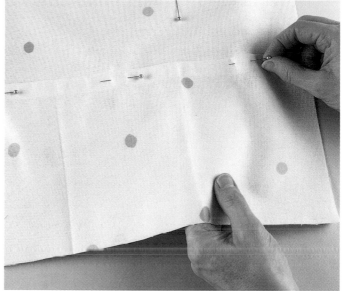

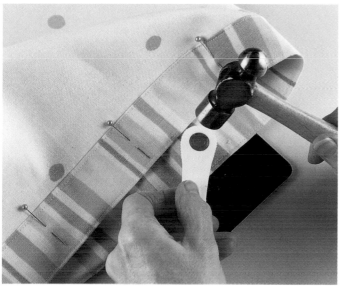

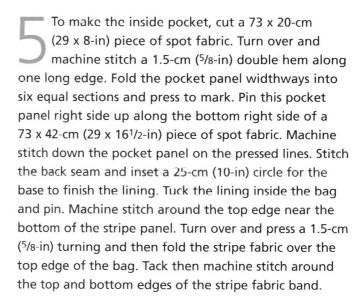

4 To make the top binding, cut a 73 x 11-cm (29 x 4³/₄-in) strip of stripe fabric so that the stripes are vertical along the length. Fold it in half widthways, machine stitch the seam and press open. Fit over the bag with right sides together so that the stripe fabric is 2.5 cm (1 in) down from the top edge and the back seams match. Machine stitch 1.5 cm (⁵/₈ in) from the top of the stripe fabric. Fold the fabric up over the top of the bag and press. Turn under 1.5 cm (⁵/₈ in) around the top edge and press.

5 To make the inside pocket, cut a 73 x 20-cm (29 x 8-in) piece of spot fabric. Turn over and machine stitch a 1.5-cm (⁵/₈-in) double hem along one long edge. Fold the pocket panel widthways into six equal sections and press to mark. Pin this pocket panel right side up along the bottom right side of a 73 x 42-cm (29 x 16¹/₂-in) piece of spot fabric. Machine stitch down the pocket panel on the pressed lines. Stitch the back seam and inset a 25-cm (10-in) circle for the base to finish the lining. Tuck the lining inside the bag and pin. Machine stitch around the top edge near the bottom of the stripe panel. Turn over and press a 1.5-cm (⁵/₈-in) turning and then fold the stripe fabric over the top edge of the bag. Tack then machine stitch around the top and bottom edges of the stripe fabric band.

6 Mark the position of the eyelets with pins around the top edge of the bag in the centre of the stripe panel. Space the eyelets evenly about 8–9cm (3–3¹/₂ in) apart, beginning with two eyelets 4 cm (1¹/₂ in) in from either side of the back seam. Insert the eyelets following the manufacturer's instructions. Thread the cord through the eyelets from one side of the back seam and round to the last hole. Feed the ends through the toggle made in Step 2 then thread the ends through the bottom tab. Check the length of the cord so that the bag can open fully and secure with a knot.

organza tote bag

A combination of appliqué, embroidery and beadwork is used to create the design on this delicate little bag. It is made from contrasting shades of silk organza and the bag constructed with French seams so that there are no raw edges inside. This bag is very easy to make and the appliqué decoration so simple that you could create your own motifs for a unique design. Use pretty pastels and white or cream to make stunning bags for bridesmaids or even the bride.

materials

- 32 x 30 cm (12½ x 12 in) bronze metallic silk organza
- 32 x 70 cm (12½ x 27½ in) pink silk organza
- Pencil
- Fusible bonding web
- Pale pink and bronze stranded cotton
- 4 oval pearl beads

Seam allowances are 1.5 cm (⅝ in) and machine stitch is straight stitch.

1   Cut two 16 x 20-cm (6¼ x 8-in) pieces of each colour of organza and put one set aside. Lay the two colours from one set one on top of the other with right sides facing and machine stitch along one long edge to make the seam. Press the seam towards the darker fabric and trim it neatly to 6 mm (¼ in). Repeat with the other set to make a second panel. Photocopy the template on page 88. Lay one panel on the template, right side up so that the seam is level with the central horizontal line and the bronze part of the fabric is below the line. Lightly trace the stems onto the fabric with a pencil.

2   Trace the leaf shapes on to fusible bonding web and iron on to scraps of bronze organza then cut out the shapes. Now trace the squares on to fusible bonding web and iron on to scraps of pink organza then cut out the shapes. Iron a second piece of pink organza on the reverse side of the squares so that they will show up against the darker fabric. When all the shapes have been cut out, peel off the backing paper and stick them in place on the right side of the marked panel. Cover the area with a piece of non-stick baking parchment to protect the iron and press to fix in place.

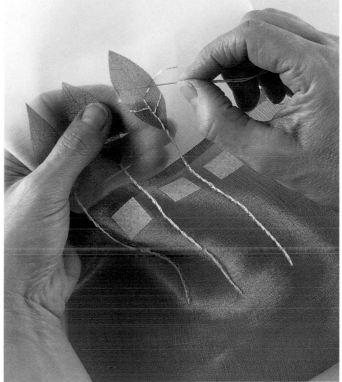

3 Using two strands of pale pink cotton, work stem stitch along each stem. To work stem stitch, bring the thread up at the bottom of the stem. Take a 4–5 mm (¹/₈–¹/₄ in) straight stitch and then bring the needle out halfway back down the stitch on one side. Continue making stitches the same length and bringing the needle out at the top of the previous stitch. Make sure your length of cotton is long enough to sew the entire stem in one go.

4 The remaining embroidery is all worked in a combination of backstitch and holbein stitch which both look the same from the right side. With holbein stitch, you work a line of running stitch and then go back to fill in the gaps to create a solid line. With backstitch you work the line as you go, bringing the needle out a stitch length in front and taking the needle back through at the top of the previous stitch. Work the leaf veins in holbein stitch then work the leaf and square edges in backstitch.

tip

When embroidering on see-through fabric avoid taking the thread across the back and always work along previous stitch lines.

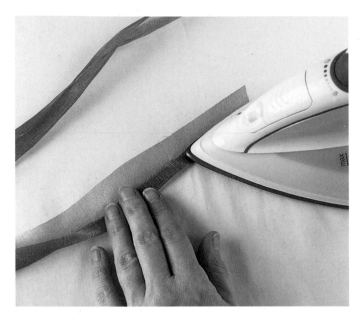

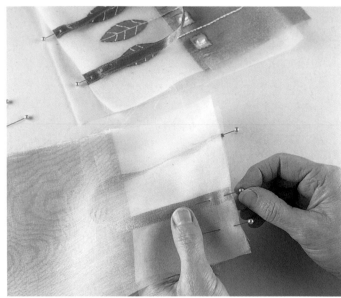

5 To make the handles, cut two 4 x 30-cm (1½ x 12-in) strips of bronze organza. Press the strips in half lengthways then fold the edges into the centre and press. Stitch close to the edge down each side of the straps in a matching thread colour. Pin the handles to the top edge of the bag panels directly above the leaves so that the raw edges are together.

6 Cut two 18 x 23-cm (7 x 9-cm) pieces of pink organza and pin these lining pieces to the right side of the bag panels. Trim the bag panels to the same size. Machine stitch across the top of the bag panels, trim the seam to 6 mm (¼ in), fold over and press.

7 To work a French seam, pin the two bag panels together with the right sides facing out. Stitch a 7-mm (³/8-in) seam along the sides and bottom. Trim the seams to 3 mm (1/8 in) and trim across the corners. Turn the bag through and press. Machine stitch a 6-mm (1/4-in) seam along the sides and bottom then turn back through to the right side and press. Finally, stitch an oval pearl bead in the centre of each square to finish.

tote with side loops

Everyone has at least one ordinary tote bag at home as they are without doubt the most useful bags. This stunning bag is just a plain tote bag with added loops at each side to give it a more interesting shape. Polka dot fabric is the ideal choice as it complements the covered buttons, but of course it would work in all sorts of fabric. If you prefer a tote with long handles to go over your shoulder, simply measure the length required and cut the strap fabric slightly longer.

materials

- 50 cm (½ yd) of 142-cm (56-in) wide blue spot fabric
- 50 cm (½ yd) of 90-cm (36-in) wide white linen, for the lining
- Knitting needle or rouleaux turner
- Two 19-mm (¾-in) self-cover buttons

Seam allowances are 1.5 cm (⅝ in) and machine stitch is straight stitch.

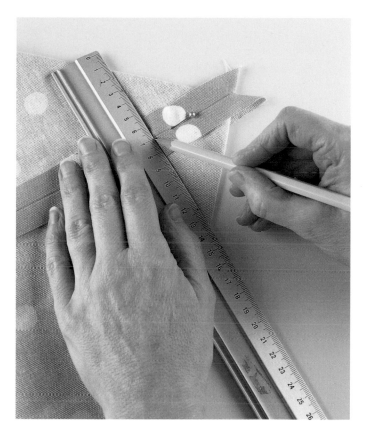

1 Cut two 45 x 46-cm (17¾ x 18-in) panels from blue spot fabric. With right sides together, machine stitch the sides and bottom seams and press open the seams. To shape the bag, open out the bottom corner, line up the bottom seam with the side seam and insert a pin through the two seams to line them up. Measure 6 cm (2⅜ in) in from the point and draw a pencil line perpendicular to the seam. Machine stitch along the line, reverse stitching at each end for strength. Repeat with the other corner then turn the bag through.

tip

to give the bag more stability, you could make a base panel from acrylic or stiff card to fit in the base before fitting the lining.

2 To make the rouleaux for the side loops, cut two 5 x 50-cm (2 x 20-in) strips of white linen. Fold each in half lengthways and machine stitch down the centre of the folded strips and across one end. Turn the strips through with the help of a knitting needle or rouleaux turner (see Techniques, page 15). Pull the inside seam allowances from each end to straighten and press with the seam down one side.

3 Fold the rouleaux from Step 2 in half widthways, open out to form a point and press. Machine stitch across the base of the triangle to secure. Machine stitch back and forwards several times across the rouleaux 2.5 cm (1 in) from the previous stitching to make a buttonhole. Turn under the ends of the side loops so that they measure 20 cm (8 in) from the fold to the point. Measure 13.5 cm (5¼ in) in from the side seams on both sides of the bag and mark with a pin. Measure down a further 11.5 cm (4½ in) and pin the folded ends at these marks on the back of the bag. Machine stitch in a square, going over the stitching a second time for strength.

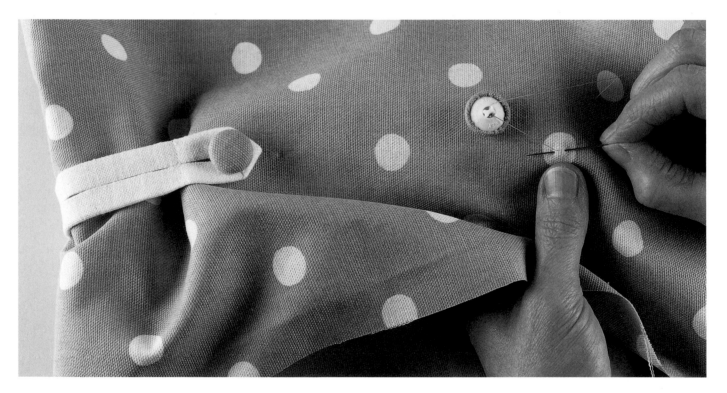

tip

take care when cutting out bag pieces from large spot fabric so that the spots are straight and match where possible.

4 Measure 8 cm (3 in) from the folded end of the side loops and pin at this point to the side seam, 11.5 cm (4½ in) down from the top edge. Stitch up and down the side seam to secure. Following the manufacturer's instructions cover the two buttons with blue fabric. Stitch the buttons at the pin marks on the front of the bag and fasten the side loops.

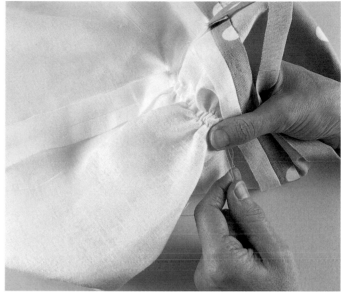

5 To make the handles, cut two 6 x 45-cm (2¼ x 18-in) strips of blue spot fabric. Fold each in half lengthways with right sides facing and machine stitch with a 6-mm (¼-in) seam allowance, stitching across one end. Turn the strips through with a knitting needle or rouleaux turner. Press the straps with the seam down one side. Measure 13.5 cm (5¼ in) in from the side seams on both sides of the bag and mark with a pin. Pin the straps at the top of the bag with the raw edges together.

6 To make the lining, cut two 10 x 45-cm (4 x 18-in) strips of blue spot fabric and two pieces of white linen, 38 x 45 cm (15 x 18 in). Machine stitch the spot fabric to the white linen to make two panels and press open the seams. Leaving a gap on one side seam for turning, make up the lining in the same way as the bag in Step 1. Mark the loop points with pins and work two rows of gathering stitches between the marks. Pull up the gathers to measure 20 cm (8 in) and tie off securely on the reverse side.

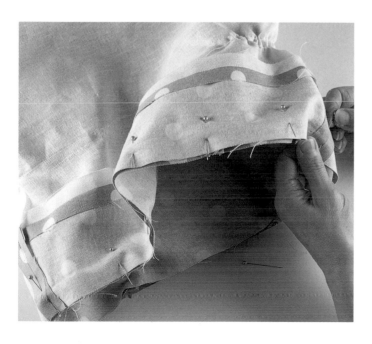

7 With right sides together, pin the strip of spot fabric from Step 6 on the white linen lining. Pin this in turn to the bag around the top edge and machine stitch. Turn the bag through and slip stitch the gap. Press the top seam.

long-handled tote

Choose a plain, canvas-style fabric with a matching print in a lighter-weight fabric for the lining to make this stunning tote bag. The bag is very easy to make but its success depends on making both layers exactly the same size so you will need to take care when marking the seam allowances and cutting out. If you can't find buckles this exact size, adjust the width of the straps and the bag pattern to suit.

materials

- 50 cm (½ yd) of 142-cm (56-in) wide deep pink canvas
- 50 cm (½ yd) of 142-cm (56-in) wide cream fabric with a pink floral pattern, for the lining
- Four 32-mm (1¼-in) silver buckles
- 15-cm (6-in) square of fusible bonding web
- Thirty six 4-mm (³/16-in) silver eyelets

Seam allowances are 1.5 cm (⅝ in) and machine stitch is straight stitch.

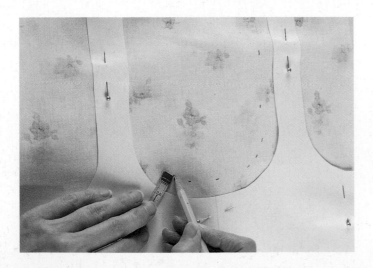

1 Photocopy then cut out the bag panel template on page 89 and cut out two pattern pieces from each colour of fabric. For the gusset, cut one 12 x 104-cm (4¾ x 41-in) strip from each colour. As it is important to have accurate seam allowances with this bag design, measure and mark the seam allowances with a pencil before cutting out (see Techniques, pages 10–11). In this case, you will achieve more accurate results by adding the seam allowance to the fabric, as shown.

2 Pin the deep pink canvas gusset around the sides of one of the deep pink bag panels, right sides together. Make 1-cm (1/2-in) snips into the gusset seam allowance to help the fabric bend around the curved shapes. Trim the gusset to the level of the top of the bag if required. Machine stitch the seam then pin and machine stitch the second deep pink canvas bag panel to the other side. Make up the lining in the same way using the pink floral fabric, leaving a gap along the bottom edge of one seam for turning. Press open the seams and trim to 6 mm (1/4 in).

tip

notch the curved corners on the lining and bag panels before joining together to ensure a perfect fit.

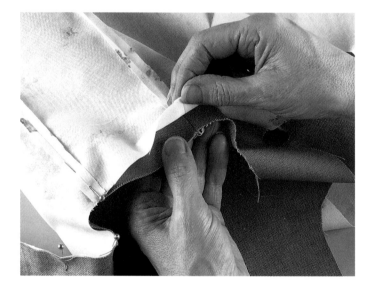

3 With right sides together, tuck the main bag inside the lining. Match the seams and pin the two layers together. Measure across the strap sections and mark the seam allowances – the gap between the seams should be 2 mm (1/32 in) wider than the inside measurement of the buckle. Machine stitch around the seams, leaving the short strap sections open at the top.

4 Trim the seams to 6 mm (1/4 in). Snip every 7 mm (3/8 in) around the curved edges. To make the strap loops, cut four 3 x 10 cm (11/8 x 4 in) pieces of pink canvas and iron fusible bonding web on the reverse of each piece. Fold right sides together widthways and machine stitch the seam. Trim the seam and press open carefully. Turn the outside raw edges to the middle and press to secure. Turn the loops through and set aside.

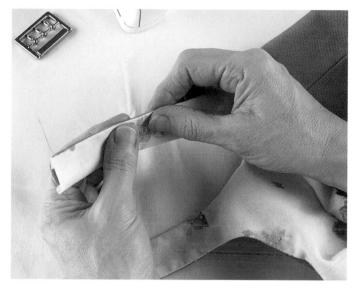

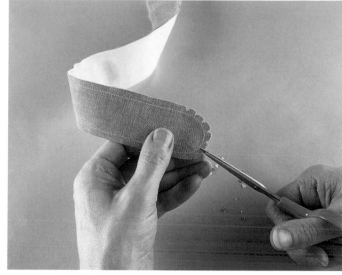

5 Turn the bag through using the gap in the lining. Roll the seams between your fingers (see Techniques, page 15) so that the seam is exactly on the edge before pressing. Slip stitch the gap in the lining. Fit the strap loops made in Step 4 over each short strap section. Tuck one of the short strap sections on the main bag over the bottom bar of the buckle. On the reverse side, fold under the raw edges and pin to make a 2.5-cm (1-in) turning. Machine stitch along the fold, and again as close to the buckle as the machine presser foot will allow.

6 For the straps, cut two 6.5 x 75-cm (2½ x 30-in) strips in each colour. With right sides together, pin the pink canvas to the floral fabric and draw a curve at each end. To ensure the straps are exactly the right width for the buckle, you can measure and mark the seam lines with a pencil and ruler. Add 2 mm (1/32 in) to the inside measurement of the buckle. Stitch along the strap and around the curves, leaving a gap for turning on one long side. Trim the seams to 6 mm (1/4 in) and then notch the curved ends, as shown in the picture. Turn the strap through, roll the seams and press carefully. Slip stitch the gap. Make a second strap in the same way.

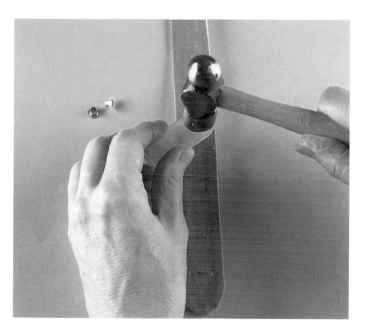

7 The number of eyelets used will depend on the number of prongs on the buckle. For a three-prong buckle, mark the position of the first set of three eyelets about 14 cm (5½ in) in from each end of the straps. Following the manufacturer's instructions, punch three holes in a row across the width of the strap and insert the eyelets to fit the prongs of the buckles. Insert another row of three eyelets 7.5 cm (3 in) above and below the first set for decoration. Finally, feed the straps into the buckles and fasten on the middle set of eyelets at each end. Tuck the ends of the straps into the strap loops.

embellished handbag

Sometimes when out shopping you might come across an inexpensive ready-made bag in a boutique or charity shop. The bag may not be made from attractive fabric or be a suitable shape or colour, but it is often worth buying for the handles alone. These lovely wood handles were one such find and the bag was redesigned to give it a more contemporary look. Embellish the bag with beads, a brooch or silk flowers.

materials

41 x 48-cm (16 x 19-in) of patterned, medium-weight
  furnishing fabric
12-mm (1-in) double-sided tape
Pair of wooden handles with a 21.5-cm (8½-in) slot
Sewing thread and fine sewing needle
Assortment of coloured beads
50 x 50-cm (20 x 20-in) of blue polyester, for the lining

Seam allowances are 1.5 cm (⅝ in) and machine stitch is straight stitch.

tip
if you choose a lightweight fabric, iron a heavy interfacing on the
reverse side before making up the bag so that it holds its shape.

1 Lay the patterned fabric piece face up. To mark the position of the tucks at the top of the bag, measure and mark the following points with pins. From both sides of one short edge, insert a pin 5 cm (2 in) in from the edges, then 3 cm (1⅛ in), 2 cm (¾ in), 3 cm (1⅛ in), 2 cm (¾ in) and 3 cm (1⅛ in) to leave a 5-cm (2-in) section in the middle. Fold the bag panel in half widthways and make a 6-mm (¼-in) snip through both layers at each pin. Remove the pins and unfold.

tip

you could easily make a larger bag by adding 20 cm (8 in) to the length of the fabric and make up in the same way.

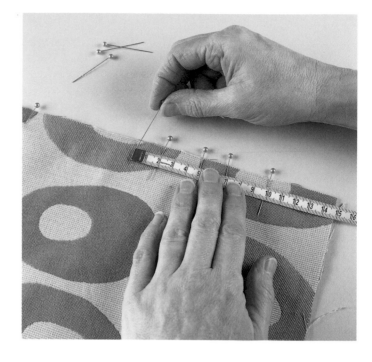

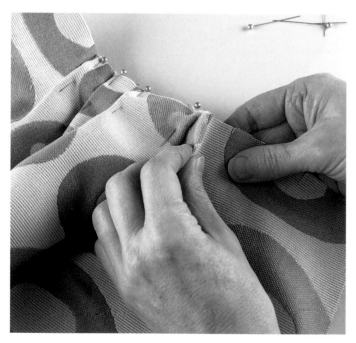

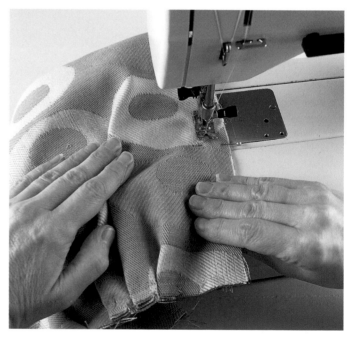

2 Now make the tucks. Beginning on one side of the 5-cm (2-in) centre section, fold a pleat in the fabric so that the two adjacent snips lay one on top of the other, and pin. Leave a gap and make the next pleat and pin; then leave a gap and make a third pleat and pin. Repeat on the other side then pleat the other end of the bag panel to match.

3 Machine stitch across the pleats, 7 mm (⅜ in) in from the raw edge, removing the pins as you go. Fold the bag right sides together and pin the side seams. Stitch up 12 cm (4¾ in) from the fold on each side, reverse stitching at the top of the seam for strength. Press the seams and the seam allowances flat on both sides.

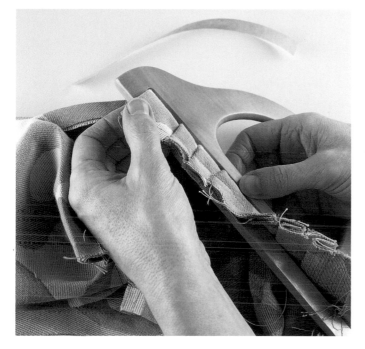

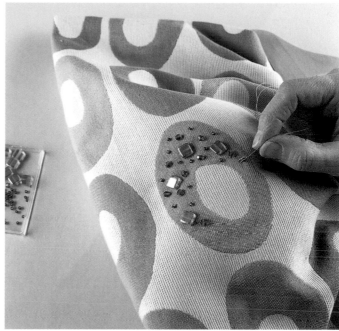

4 Stick double-sided tape on the inside of the wooden handles underneath the slot. Feed the pleated fabric into the slot from the outside of both handles. Peel off the tape's backing paper and fold the fabric onto the tape. You will need to pull more fabric through towards the outside so that the fabric fills the slots.

5 Embellish the bag with beads. With this fabric, the beads pick out one of the oval motifs on the front of the bag. To stitch on the beads, tie a large knot on the end of a double length of thread and bring it out to the front of the fabric. Pick up a bead and take the thread back through to the other side. Take a second stitch through the bead for security. Continue adding beads with two stitches each time until the embellishment is complete. Secure the thread with two small backstitches on the reverse side.

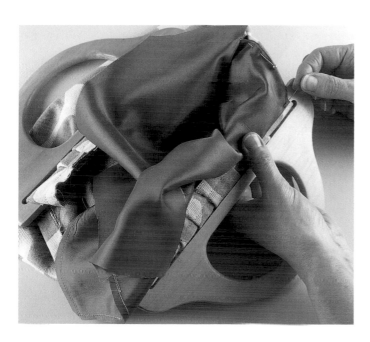

6 Lay the bag down in the middle of a piece of folded lining fabric. Cut around the sides and base of the bag, leaving a 1.5-cm (5/8-in) seam allowance. Leave ample seam allowance along the top edge. Mark the position of the side seam on the lining with pins. Machine stitch the side and bottom seams between the pins and trim to 6 mm (1/4 in). Tuck the lining into the bag and pin the side seams. Fold over the top edge of the lining neatly and pin it to the tucks as close as possible to the slit of the handle. Stitch the lining into the bag with slip stitch so that the stitches are almost invisible.

reversible bag

Reversible clothing has the advantage of giving you two different looks for the price of one garment and this unusual bag has the same effect. The buttons allow you to take the bag off the handles and turn it outside in to change the colour emphasis. You could of course change the handles too! Choose two fabrics that tone in together and match the buttons to the handles to create a co-ordinating design.

materials

- 50 cm (20in) of 90-cm (36-in) wide lilac fabric
- 50 cm (20in) of 90-cm (36-in) wide lilac patterned fabric
- 50 cm (20 in) of 7-mm (3/8-in) wide purple organza ribbon
- Pair of 19.5-cm (7¾-in) wide black acrylic handles
- Twelve 2–2.5-cm (¾–1-in) buttons

Seam allowances are 1.5 cm (5/8 in) and machine stitch is straight stitch.

1 Photocopy the template on page 90 and cut two bag panels and one 9 x 65-cm (3$\frac{1}{2}$ x 25$\frac{1}{2}$-in) strip from both fabrics. To make the gussets, lay out the strips then measure and mark 15 cm (6 in) down each side from each end. Mark the centre point on the ends of each strip. Draw pencil lines from the centre point to the 15-cm (6-in) marks to create a point and cut along the lines, gently curving into the side edges.

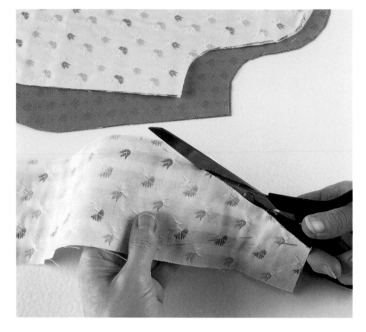

tip

mark the seam allowances on the fabric before cutting out so that both layers are the same size.

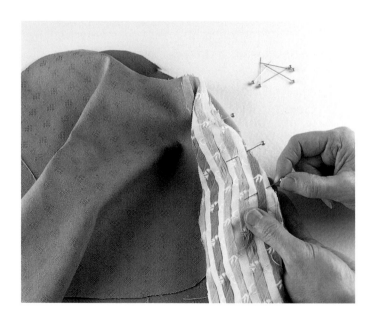

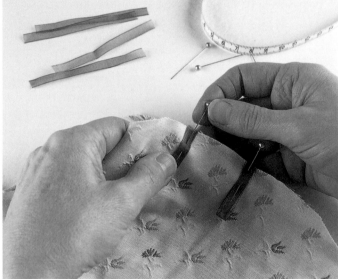

2 Pin the lilac bag panels together with right sides facing and machine stitch a 4-cm (1$\frac{1}{2}$-in) long seam down from the top edge at each side, reverse stitching for strength. Press open the seams. Pin the patterned gusset in place on one side of the lilac bag panel. Machine stitch from point to point then pin and stitch the second side. Make up the patterned bag panels with a plain lilac gusset in the same way, leaving a gap along the straight bottom edge for turning through.

3 Cut six 8-cm (3-in) lengths of purple ribbon and fold each in half widthways. Pin one folded ribbon in the centre top of one patterned bag panel with the raw edges together and the loop facing down into the bag. Pin a folded piece of ribbon 3.5 cm (1$\frac{3}{8}$ in) on either side. Pin the remaining three strips of ribbon in the same place on the other side of the bag.

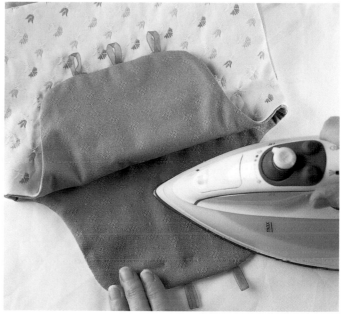

4 Turn the lilac bag inside out and leave the patterned bag right side out. Tuck the patterned bag inside the lilac bag with right sides together and pin around the top edge, matching the seams. Stitch around the edge. Trim the seam allowance to 6 mm (¹/₄ in). Notch the outer curves then carefully snip the inner curves (see Techniques, page 14).

5 Turn through the gap on the patterned fabric bag and press carefully. To get the seam exactly on the edge, dampen your fingers and roll the seam (see Techniques, page 15). Slip stitch the gap.

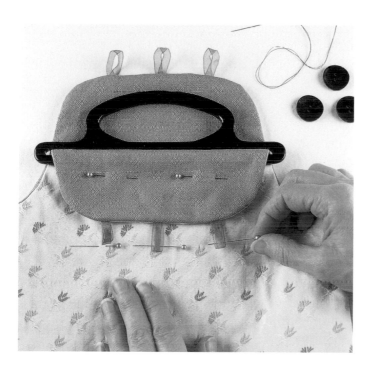

6 Fit the handles and pin the flap in position. To mark the positions of the buttons, insert pins about 3 mm (¹/₈ in) from the bottom of the ribbon loops. Sew one set of buttons on each side of the bag. To make the bag reversible, sew another two sets of buttons on top of the previous buttons, stitching on the inside of the bag.

tip
you can use one set of buttons for the patterned fabric and another for the plain fabric side if you prefer.

corduroy work bag

With knitting proving an ever-popular pastime, this useful workbag is stylish enough to take into work so that you can catch up with your knitting at lunchtime. It has been cleverly designed with two overlapping diagonal panels that create pockets on both the outside and the inside. The bag could be made in all one colour, but the two contrasting colours emphasize the attractive diagonal lines that also create the gap for the bamboo handle. Choose a sturdy fabric such as this fine needlecord, or even denim or canvas to make a practical bag with lots of room for your work and plenty of spaces to keep scissors and other paraphernalia safe.

materials

50 cm (½ yd) of 90cm (36in) thin-ribbed (needlecord) cream corduroy
50 cm (½ yd) of 90cm (36in) thin-ribbed (needlecord) rust corduroy
Pencil
Two 32-cm (12½-in) bamboo rods
Sewing thread in cream and rust

Seam allowances are 1.5 cm (⅝ in) and machine stitch is straight stitch.

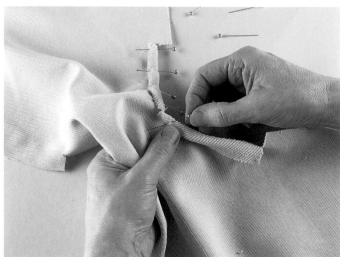

1 Fold the cream corduroy fabric in half so that the ribs are perpendicular to the fold. Photocopy then cut out the bag panel template on page 91 and pin the pattern on the cream fabric so that the top edge is on the fold. Add 1.5 cm (5/8 in) seam allowances to the other sides and cut out. Cut out two bag panels in each colour in the same way.

2 Mark the dots shown on the template with a pencil on all four pattern pieces. These marks indicate where to stitch. Remove the paper pattern and snip 1.5 cm (5/8 in) into the marked dots. Open out the cream fabric panel. At the top of the diagonal edge, fold the seam allowance in half between the marked dots then fold over to the reverse side and pin. The turning will narrow towards the middle but you should turn over enough to catch when you stitch along the edge. Machine stitch next to the fold and again along the edge of the turning.

3 Fold the cream fabric panel along the fold line marked on the template with right sides together and stitch the diagonal seam. Stitch the side seam down as far as the marked dot. Trim the seams and press open. Turn the panel through and pin the diagonal seam. Top stitch this seam with two rows of stitching, continuing down from the previous stitching. Make all four panels in the same way.

4 Overlap a cream and a rust panel so that the cream is on the top. Insert a bamboo rod handle in the folds and pin the layers together. Use a saucer approximately 13 cm (5 in) in diameter to draw curves in each bottom corner to shape the bag. Pin and tack all layers together. Thread the sewing machine with cream thread on the top and rust thread in the bobbin. Machine stitch a diamond shape along the previous stitching lines to sew the two panels together where they cross. Make a second bag panel in exactly the same way.

5 For the gusset, cut an 18 x 78-cm (7 x 30³/4-in) strip of rust corduroy. Turn under a narrow turning at each end of the strip and machine stitch. With right sides facing, pin one side of the gusset to the first bag panel. Snip into the gusset seam allowance to ease the fabric around the curve more easily. Machine stitch and then attach the second bag panel to the other side.

tip

when fitting the gusset, mark the centre on the bag and gusset and match these points before pinning the sides.

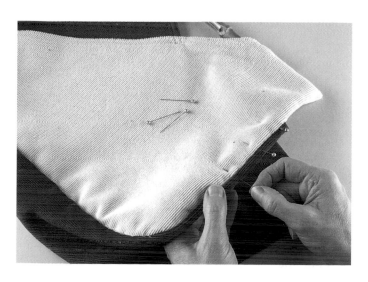

6 The raw edges on this bag are self-bound using the gusset fabric. To do this, trim the seams accurately to 6 mm (¹/4 in) and turn the bag through. Fold over the top edge of the gusset and trim off the corners to reduce bulk. On one side, fold the gusset back over the trimmed seam and pin so that the raw edges are enclosed. If you prefer, tack and remove the pins then machine stitch along the edge of the binding from the right side. Repeat the process on the back of the bag.

ribbon and canvas shopper

This brightly coloured bag has large, useful pockets that make it ideal for keeping lots of bits and bobs. It is the perfect size to take on a picnic or for a day on the beach. The bag is interfaced using an iron-on canvas interfacing sold for heavy tailoring. This helps to support the weight of the acrylic handles. You could also make fabric handles and extend the lime ribbon to strengthen. The bag can be made any colours you want – just pick one grosgrain ribbon to tone in with the fabric and another for contrast.

materials

- 90 cm (36 in) of 145-cm (57-in) wide green cotton canvas
- 46 cm (18 in) of 90-cm (36-in) wide iron-on canvas interfacing
- Sewing threads to match the fabric and ribbons
- 2 m (2 yd) of 2.5-cm (1-in) wide aubergine grosgrain ribbon
- 2 m (2 yd) of 1.5-cm (⅝-in) wide lime grosgrain ribbon
- Pair of green acrylic handles, 14 cm (5½ in) wide at the base

Seam allowances are 1.5 cm (⅝ in) and machine stitch is straight stitch.

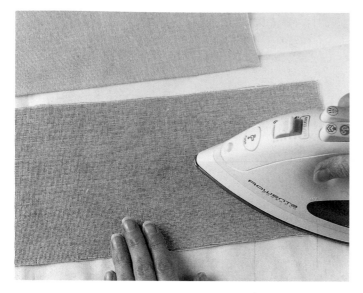

1   Cut two pieces of green canvas, 34 x 91 cm (13½ x 36 in) for the main bag and one piece of interfacing the same size. Cut another piece of green canvas, 20 x 91 cm (8 x 36 in) for the pocket. Cut two green canvas base panels, 15 x 35 cm (6 x 13¾ in), and one piece of interfacing the same size. Iron the interfacing to the reverse side of the matching canvas pieces.

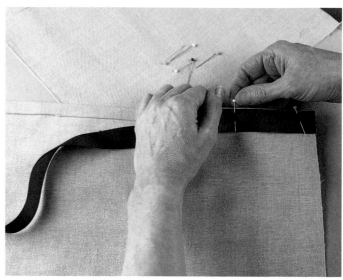

2   On one of the interfaced bag panels, press a 1.5-cm (⅝-in) turning to the right side along one long edge. Pin the aubergine ribbon along the top edge to cover the turning and machine stitch down each edge of the ribbon in the same direction to prevent it warping. Press the same size of turning to the right side of the pocket panel and machine stitch a length of aubergine ribbon along the turning to cover the raw edges.

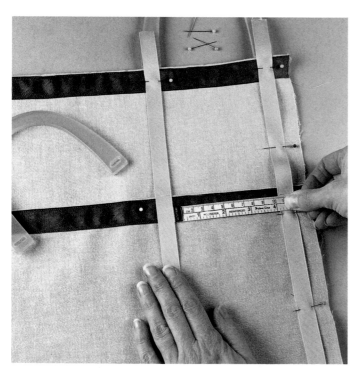

			handle position				handle position
9 cm	12 cm	9 cm	14 cm	9 cm	12 cm	9 cm	14 cm
			← 32 cm →				
1.5 cm seam allowance			pocket panel				1.5 cm seam allowance

3   Pin the pocket panel to the front of the bag panel so that the bottom edges align. Insert pins along the top and bottom edges as shown on the diagram above to mark the position of ribbons, handles and corners. Position one handle at the right-hand side, level with the seam allowance. Pin the lime ribbon directly down from each side of the handle, leaving 6 cm (2½ in) jutting up above the bag edge.

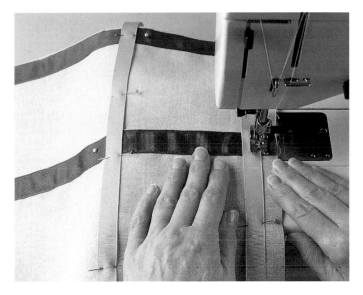

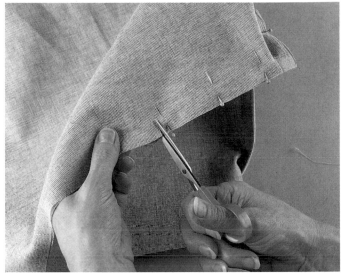

4 Position the second handle between the other 14-cm (5½-in) marks on the left of the diagram and pin lime ribbon as before. Machine stitch down each edge of the ribbon, reverse stitching at the top of each length for strength. Fold the bag widthways right sides together. Stitch the back seam of the bag, making sure that the aubergine ribbons align horizontally. Trim away the interfacing from the seam allowance and press open the seam.

5 With right sides together, pin one of the interfaced base panels between the 32-cm (12½-in) marks. Machine stitch between the pins, reverse stitching at each end for strength. Work around the base panel stitching one side at a time. Snip into the seam at each pin mark to make it easier to turn the corner and stitch.

6 Make a lining from the remaining bag and base panels. Pin the base into the bag panel so that the back seam will match when the lining is tucked inside. Trim the base panel seams and press a 1.5-cm (5/8-in) turning to the outside along the top edge. Tuck the lining into the bag. Feed the ribbon tabs through the handles and tack securely. Pin the lining in position and machine stitch around the top edge. Remember to match the thread colour in the machine to the ribbon and the fabric.

tip

for a more professional finish, match the top machine thread to the ribbon and the bobbin thread to the fabric.

dalmatian print and marabou feathers

The style of this bag is classic and it can easily be made either as a handbag, or if the pattern is enlarged, you can make a shopping bag instead. The choice of fabric is quite personal, but animal prints are never really out of fashion. This Dalmatian print is rather fun and you can add a touch of opulence with a luxurious marabou feather trim. Of course, marabou feather is just one option for trimming – you could use ruched ribbon, silk flowers or bead trim to embellish the bag.

materials

- 50 cm (½ yd) of 90-cm (36-in) wide animal print fabric
- 50 cm (½ yd) of 90-cm (36-in) wide canvas iron-on fusible interfacing
- 50 cm (½ yd) of 90-cm (36-in) wide fusible tieback interfacing, optional
- 50 cm (½ yd) of 90-cm (36-in) wide black cotton poplin, for the lining
- 32 cm (12 in) of 7-mm (⅜-in) wide black ribbon
- Pair of 8 x 14 cm (3¼ x 5½ in) black acrylic handles
- Magnetic clasp and epoxy resin, optional
- 75 cm (30 in) black Marabou feather trim

Seam allowances are 1.5 cm (⅝ in) and machine stitch is straight stitch.

dalmatian print and marabou feathers

1 Photocopy then cut out the templates on page 92. Pin the bag panel template to the animal print fabric so that the pile is running down the bag and, adding seam allowances all round, cut two bag panels and one base panel. Cut the iron-on interfacing to the same size and iron it onto the reverse of each bag and base panel. Mark the corner points on the base and bag panels with tailor tacks (see Techniques, page 11).

tip

if you can't find fusible stiff interfacing you can spray the pieces with adhesive and stick in place in the bag instead.

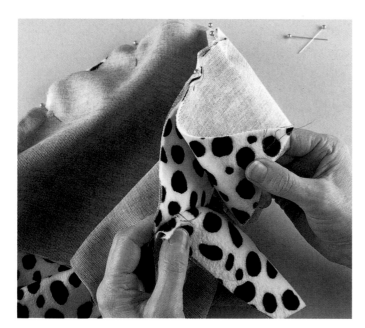

2 Pin the bag panels, right side together. Machine stitch the side seams, reverse stitching at the first tailor tacks for strength. Insert the base panel, matching the tailor tacks to those on the bag panels. Machine stitch one side at a time, stitching from point to point, reverse stitching at each end. Notch the corners and trim the ends of the points on the base panel.

3 This step is optional. It is slightly fiddly but does give the bag a very firm shape. Cut fusible tieback interfacing the exact size of the pattern pieces. Turn the bag through and insert the base panel. Use a rolled towel to support the shape and press to secure. Turn the bag through, insert the two side panels so that they tuck under the seam allowances, then iron in place. Fold the fabric over the stiff interfacing around the top edge and machine stitch.

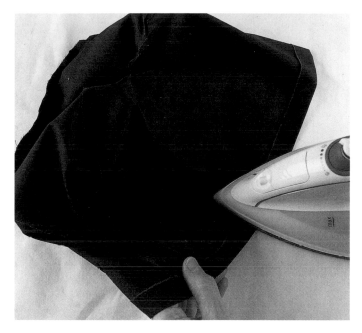

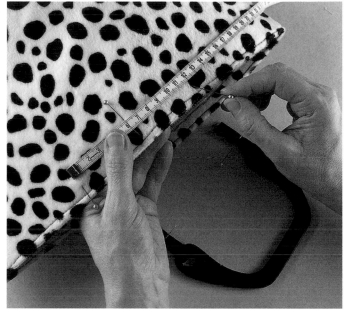

4 Cut two bag lining panels and a base panel from black cotton poplin. If you like, make a small pocket and attach to one side of the lining (see Step 5 page 79). Machine stitch the lining together in the same way as the bag. Press open the seams and turn down 1.5 cm (⅝ in) around the top edge.

5 Feed an 8-cm (3-in) piece of black ribbon through each of the handle holes. Pin the ribbon on the inside of the bag so that the handles are central. Don't make the ribbon too tight – the handles should be able to move up and down. Machine stitch two or three times along the previous seam line to secure.

tip

when fitting a magnetic clasp, iron a square of medium-weight interfacing on the reverse side of the fabric or lining to help support the weight of the fastening.

6 Tuck the lining inside the bag and pin. If you want to add a magnetic clasp, fit it now through the lining and use strong glue such as epoxy resin to stick the fastening to the stiff interfacing. Slip stitch the lining to the bag fabric. Pin the marabou feather trim around the top edge of the bag and trim to the correct length. Oversew the marabou feather neatly so that no stitches show on the inside of the bag.

pvc floral bag

This fun bag has been specially designed to make it as easy as possible to make. Rather than insetting a base panel, the box shape is simply made by folding the corners of the flat bag shape and stitching across. The handle has screw fittings so that you can add the beads of your choice, but you could, of course, use a ready-made bead handle to match the fabric. The beauty of this 'add a bead' handle is that you can choose beads that match the bag fabric exactly.

materials

- 45 x 90 cm (18 x 36 in) of floral print PVC
- Pencil
- Ruler
- Four sets of silver poppers
- Hammer
- Pair of 14 x 9.5 cm (5½ x 3¾ in) silver screw handles for beads
- Approximately thirty two 12-mm (½-in) beads
  in colours to match PVC
- Super glue or epoxy resin
- Fabric glue
- Paper clips
- Stiff card
- Spray adhesive

Seam allowances are 1.5 cm (⅝ in) and machine stitch is straight stitch.

pvc floral bag

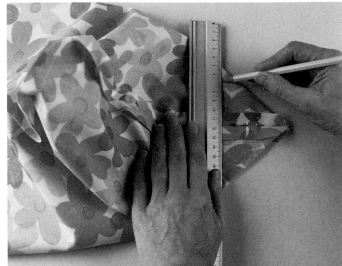

1 Cut two 35 x 33-cm (14 x 13-in) pieces of PVC. With right sides together, stitch the short side seams and the bottom seam. Reverse stitch at the top of each seam for strength. Trim across the corners.

tip

for accurately-cut bag pieces, measure and mark the PVC with a pencil on the reverse side.

2 To make the box base, open out the bottom corner, line up the bottom seam with the side seam and insert a pin through the two seams to line them up. Measure 7 cm (2³/4 in) in from the point and draw a pencil line perpendicular to the seam. Machine stitch along the line and trim to 6 mm (1/4 in). Repeat with the other corner.

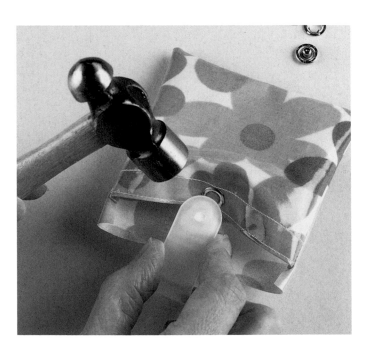

3 To make the inside pocket, cut a 12 x 20-cm (5 x 8-in) piece of PVC. Turn over 1.5 cm (5/8 in) at one short end and machine stitch two rows 1 cm (1/2 in) apart. Fold widthways with right sides together to leave 12 mm (1/2 in) above the stitched edge. Machine stitch the seams and turn through. Using a hammer and the setting tool supplied with the poppers, follow the manufacturer's instructions to insert a popper at the centre of the pocket.

tip

for a neat inside finish, you can stick down the side and bottom seams using fabric glue before stitching the corners.

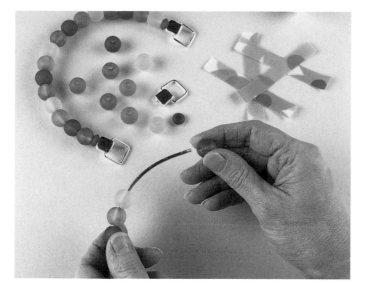

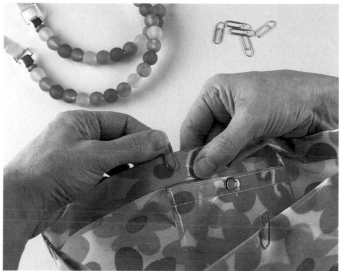

4 Unscrew one end of the bead handles, thread on sufficient beads then re-fit the fastening. You may need to use a couple of smaller spacer beads at each end to achieve a tight fit. For extra security, apply a few drops of super glue or epoxy resin to fix the screw fastening permanently. Cut four 12 mm x 8-cm (1/2 in x 3-in) strips of PVC fabric. Slot the strips through the handle holes and stick together with fabric glue.

5 Turn the bag through and turn down 2 cm (3/4 in) and then a further 2 cm (3/4 in). Hold the top hem in place with paper clips. Trim the excess seam allowance from inside the hem to reduce bulk. Tuck the pocket under the seam on one side and hold in position with paper clips. Tuck the handle tabs under and fold up so that they just clear the top edge. Machine stitch around the lower edge of the hem, removing the paper clips as you go. Stitch again around the top edge.

tip

fold a scrap of PVC to mock-up the top hem of the bag. Practise inserting poppers and check that you are fitting them the right way round. The popper fastening side should be to the outside of the bag on the side seams and facing in between the handles.

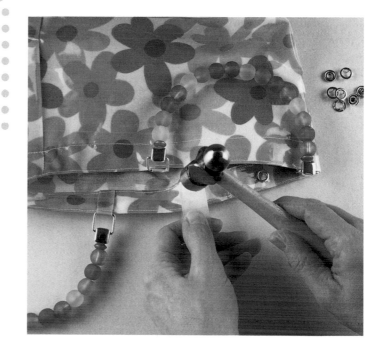

6 With a pencil, mark 3 cm (1/4 in) on both sides of the side seam in the middle of the top hem. Following the manufacturer's instructions, fit a matching set of poppers on either side of the side seams. Close the poppers to shape the bag. Mark the centre point between the handles and fit another set of poppers. Measure the base of the bag and cut a piece of stiff card to fit. Spray the card with adhesive and cover it with a slightly larger piece of PVC fabric and stick, card-side down, in the base of the bag.

gathered tweed handbag

This bag has been specially designed for round handles, whether they are acrylic, wood or bamboo. For the fabric, choose from some of the absolutely gorgeous tweeds available in a stunning range of colours and textures to match the colour of the handles. Some tweeds have novelty yarns incorporated in the weave, so take care to cut both bag panels the right way up. If you prefer a different type of fabric, choose one with a soft feel that will gather neatly around the handles.

materials

- 50 cm (½ yd) of 115-cm (45-in) wide tweed, or other soft fabric
- Pair of 18-cm (7-in) diameter round bamboo handles
- 45-cm (18-in) square piece of iron-on interfacing
- Magnetic fastener and epoxy resin
- 50 cm (½ yd) of 91-cm (36-in) wide black cotton poplin, for the lining
- Bamboo toggle
- Pliers

Seam allowances are 1.5 cm (⅝ in) and machine stitch is straight stitch.

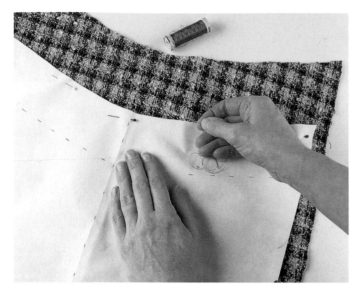

1 Photocopy the templates on page 93 and make separate pattern pieces for the bag panel, lining, tab and pocket. Fold the tweed in half widthways with right sides together. Pin the bag pattern to the fabric and, adding seam allowances all round, cut to make two bag panels. Mark the dots at each side with tailor tacks (see Techniques, page 11) and separate the two pieces. To mark the fold line at the top of each bag panel, move the template down so that it is level with the first tailor tacks down from the top edge. Tack along the curved edge on both pattern pieces.

2 Pin the bag panels with right sides facing and machine stitch around the bottom curved edge, between the two lower tailor tacks, reverse stitching at each end for strength. Stitch again 2 mm (1/16 in) from the first stitched line for strength. Trim and notch the curved edge only and then turn through to the right side.

tip

use a brightly coloured thread that will show up clearly against the tweed when tacking or inserting tailor tacks.

3 Turn under the top section of the side seam allowances and tack. With the right side facing, machine stitch close to the fold down one side, turn and go back and forwards several times across the seam to reinforce before stitching up the other side. Fold the bag panels over along the tacking line, tuck the bamboo handles inside and pin. Backstitch through both layers underneath the handles, stitching the thread ends in securely. It is easier to backstitch if you pull the pinned fabric out around the handle so that it is flat, and then gather back up once stitched.

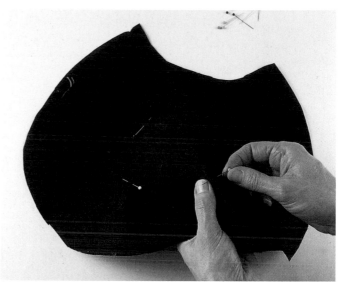

4 Cut two tab panels from the template and iron interfacing onto one tab panel. Fit the thinner side of the magnetic fastening to the interfaced panel where indicated on the template following the manufacturer's instructions. You can reinforce the fastening by sticking a 2.5-cm (1-in) square of interfacing over the back of the fastening with epoxy resin. To finish the tab, pin right sides together and machine stitch around the edge, leaving a gap for turning on one long side. Trim seams and across the corners and turn through. Pin the tab along the backstitching line on the back of the bag and mark the position of the magnetic fastening on the front of the bag. Iron a small square of interfacing on the inside for added strength and fit the thicker side of the magnetic fastening.

5 Cut two lining panels from the black cotton poplin and mark the dots with tailor tacks. Cut two lining panels from the interfacing and iron on the reverse side of the lining panels. To make the inside pocket, cut a 14-cm (5½-in) square of cotton poplin. Turn over a double 1-cm (½-in) hem at one side and machine stitch. Fold under 1 cm (½-in) on the remaining three sides and press Pin in position (refer to the template for the correct positioning) and machine stitch the three sides, reverse stitching at each end for strength.

6 Stay stitch (see Techniques, page 11) the top curves of each lining panel and then snip close to the stitching every 2 cm (¾ in). Pin the lining panels together with the pocket on the inside. Machine stitch between the tailor tacks, reverse stitching at each end for strength. Trim the curved edge only to 6 mm (¼ in). Turn under the top edge and tack. Tuck the lining inside the bag and slip stitch in place. Stitch the narrow end of the tab to the seam at the back of the bag. Stitch a bamboo toggle to the front of the tab.

beach bag

This bag is ideal for the beach as it stands up nicely so it is less likely that sand will get into your picnic, swimwear or sun cream. When making the bag, it is essential to cut the interfacing and fabrics out accurately so that the fabric outer fits the stiffly-lined inner. Don't worry if you can't get hold of blue handles to make this bag – you can simply dye clear acrylic handles with an ordinary multi-purpose household dye. It's an easy process that takes less than half an hour. See Techniques, page 17 for instructions on how to dye handles.

materials

50 cm (½ yd) fusible tieback interfacing
Pencil
50 cm (½ yd) embroidered blue gingham fabric
50 cm (½ yd) plain blue canvas fabric
Fusible bonding web
Pair of 13-cm (5-in) round blue acrylic handles

To dye clear handles:
Dylon multi-purpose hot dye to match fabric
Household salt

Seam allowances are 1.5 cm (⅝ in) and machine stitch is straight stitch.

1 If necessary, dye clear acrylic handles to match the fabric (see Techniques, page 17). Photocopy then cut out the templates on pages 94–95 and cut out two bag panels, two side panels and a base panel without seam allowances from fusible tieback interfacing. On the bag panels, draw a pencil line 3 mm (1/8 in) in from the edge along the curved line and cut along the line.

tip

to cut accurate seam allowances in fabric, draw out new pattern pieces using the template adding exactly 1.5 cm (5/8 in) all round.

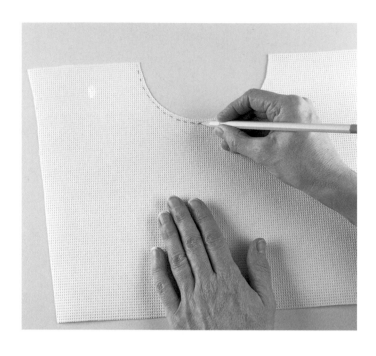

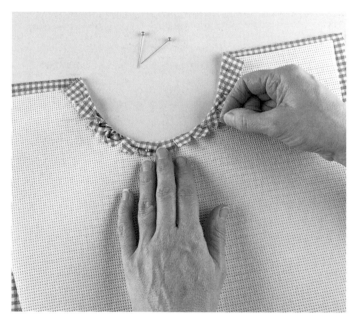

2 Adding a 1.5-cm (5/8-in) seam allowance all round, cut out two bag panels, two side panels and a base panel from the gingham fabric. Lay the template centrally on the reverse side of the gingham panels, draw along the curved lines and machine stitch exactly on the line. Iron the fusible tieback interfacing on the reverse side of the fabric panels. Snip into the machine stitching and press over the seam allowance. Tack around the curved edge.

3 Pin the bag panels together so that the gingham is on the inside and stitch the side seams. Press open the seams. Now pin the base panel in position, stitch around all sides turning neatly at each corner. Trim the base seams to 6 mm (1/4 in). You now have a stiff inner bag lining. Set aside.

4 Now make the outer bag. Adding 1.5 cm (⁵/₈ in) all round, cut two bag panels, two side panels and a base panel from the plain blue fabric. Now trim the templates along the contrast line then cut the contrast panels in gingham fabric. Press under 1.5 cm (⁵/₈ in) along the top edges of the gingham panels, pin to the plain panels so that the bottom edges align and stitch along the top edge. Machine stitch or tack around the edges inside the seam allowances to secure the layers.

5 Stay stitch the curved edges, then snip and tack. Pin the outer bag panels together and machine stitch the side seams with 12-mm (¹/₂-in) seam allowances. The smaller seam allowance makes the outer bag slightly larger to fit over the inner bag. Press open the seams and check the fit. Mark the base line, remove the outer bag and pin the outer bag base panel in position and machine stitch. Trim the base seams to 6 mm (¹/₄ in).

6 To make the tabs, cut ten 6 x 9-cm (2³/₈ x3¹/₂-in) strips from the gingham fabric and iron on to fusible bonding web. Cut the bonding web to the size of the strips. Fold the strips in three lengthways to make 2-cm (³/₄-in) wide tabs and press. Fold five tabs in half over each handle and stitch to secure in place. Pin and tack the tabs in position around the curved edges of the inner bag so that the tabs are evenly spaced. Adjust the outer bag over the stiff inner bag. Fold under the outer top edge level with the inner and pin. Machine stitch around the top edge first and then change to a zipper foot in the sewing machine so that you can stitch near the handles. Stitch around the curves carefully, reverse stitching at each end for strength.

tie feature bag

The lovely opulent quality of this handbag is achieved using a fairly heavy furnishing fabric which has an intricate floral pattern woven in the weave. This type of fabric is woven in a Jacquard loom that uses punch cards to control the warp threads and so create the design. Choose a finer plain weave fabric for the tie feature so that it gives the effect of a scarf tied casually around the bag. You can easily change the tie to co-ordinate this bag with a particular outfit for a special occasion.

materials

- 40 x 84 cm (16 x 33 in) cream jacquard weave fabric
- 40 x 54 cm (16 x 22 in) canvas interfacing
- Ruler
- Pencil
- 1 m (39 in) of 6-mm (¼-in) wide cream or white ribbon
- 16 x 32 cm (6¼ x 12½) fusible bonding web
- Pair of 9 x12-cm (3½ x 4¾-in) oval natural wood handles
- 65 x 60 cm (24 x 26 in) cream floral print fabric, for the lining

Seam allowances are 1.5 cm (⅝ in) and machine stitch is straight stitch.

1 Cut two pieces of 40 x 42-cm (16 x 16½-in) cream jacquard weave fabric, and two pieces of 40 x 27-cm (15¾ x 10½-in) canvas interfacing. Place the interfacing onto the wrong side of the cream fabric so that the bottom edges align, then iron. Repeat with the other panel. Pin the panels, right sides together, then stitch the side and bottom seams.

tip

if you want to save time and avoid tacking layers of fabric prior to machine stitching, simply insert pins across the seam and you will be able to stitch over the pins.

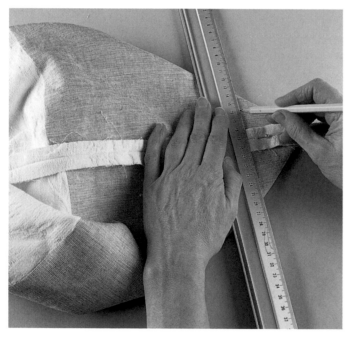

2 Press open the seams. Open out the bottom corner, line up the bottom seam with the side seam so that the side seam is on top and insert a pin through the two seams to line them up. Measure 6 cm (2⅜ in) in from the point and draw a pencil line about 12 cm (4¾ in) long perpendicular to the seam. Machine stitch along the line, reverse stitching at each end for strength. Zigzag the seam and trim off the triangle of fabric. Repeat with the other corner.

3 Trim the side seams down to the edge of the interfacing to reduce bulk. Fold over the top edge so that the side seams measure 25 cm (10 in). Machine stitch 5 cm (2 in) from the top edge and again at 6.5 cm (2½ in) to create a 15-mm (½-in) casing. On the inside, snip a few stitches between the casing lines at one side seam. Thread through the ribbon and bring both ends out the same gap. Pull up the ribbon until the bag opening measures 20 cm (8 in) across the inside of the bag and tie securely.

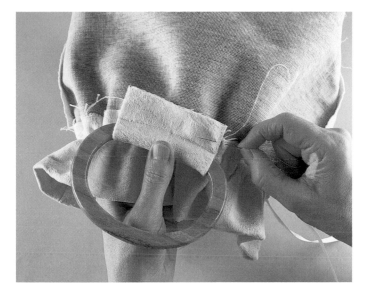

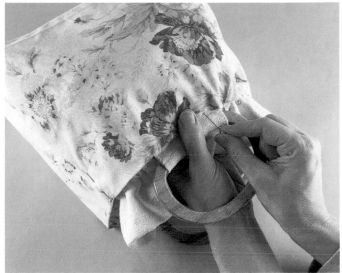

4 To make the handle tabs, cut two 16-cm (6¹/₄-in) squares of cream jacquard weave and iron fusible bonding web on the reverse side and cut to size. Fold two opposite edges into the centre and press. Fold the fabric tabs around the handles so that the raw edges are together and, with a zipper foot fitted, stitch as close to the handle as possible. Pin the handles inside the bag and stitch securely to the casing line.

5 To make the lining, cut two 40 x 22-cm (15³/₄ x 8⁵/₈-in) pieces of floral print fabric. With right sides together, sew the side and bottom seams and stitch the corners as described in Step 2. Turn the bag outside in and tuck it inside the lining. Turn under the top edge of the lining and pin, easing in to fit the gathers. Slip stitch above the casing line.

6 To make the decorative scarf, cut a 25 x 60-cm (10 x 23¹/₂-in) strip of floral print fabric. Fold the fabric in half lengthways with right sides together. Measure 25 cm (10 in) from each end along the raw edges. With a pencil, draw a curved line from this point to the fold at the end of the strip. Stitch along the line, leaving a 15-cm (6-in) gap in the middle for turning. Trim the seams, turn through and press then slip stitch the gap. Tie the scarf around the bag. Arrange the folds and gathers and pin in position. Stitch the scarf invisibly between the folds to hold the fabric in position.

tip

trim the excess fabric away from the point of the scarf and use a large knitting needle to turn the point through.

organza tote bag (pages 38–42)

Photocopy actual size

long-handled tote
(pages 48–51)

When photocopying,
enlarge by 200%

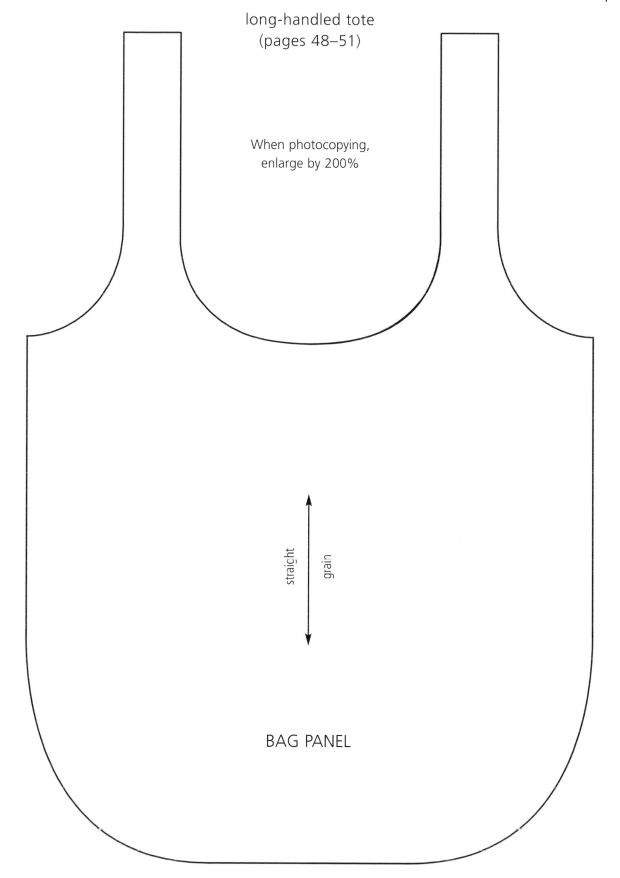

straight grain

BAG PANEL

reversible bag (pages 56–59)

When photocopying,
enlarge by 167%

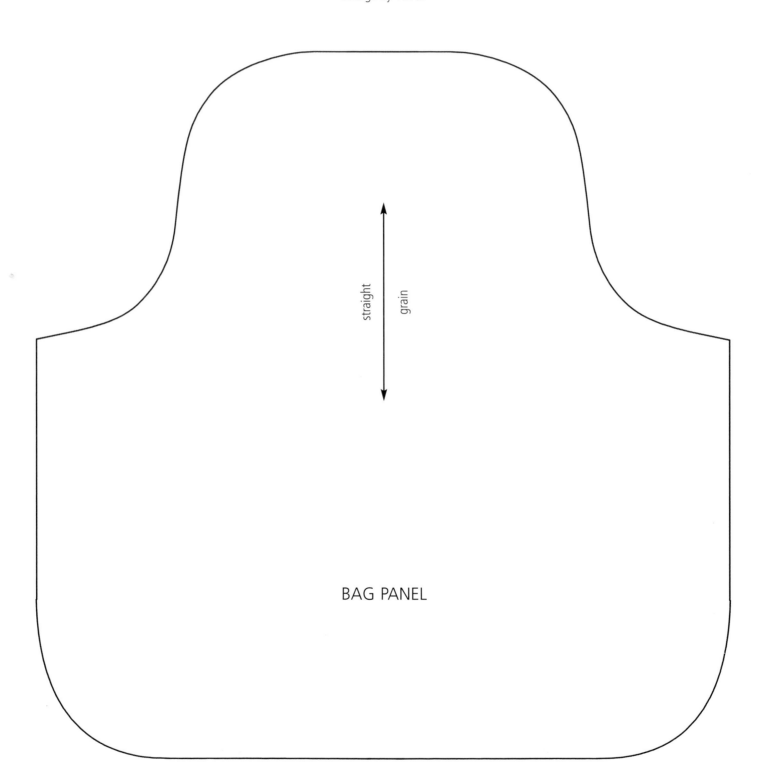

straight grain

BAG PANEL

corduroy work bag (pages 60–63)

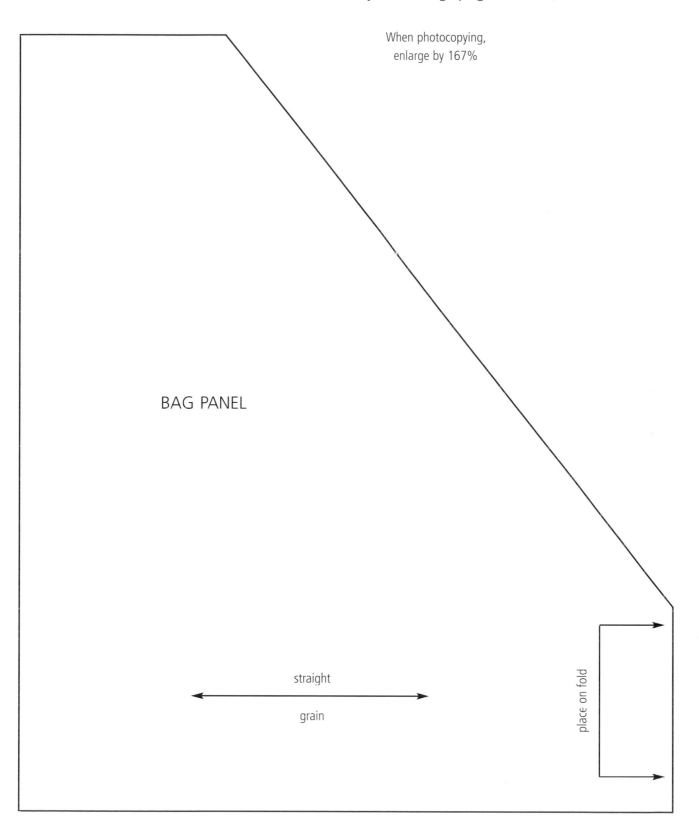

When photocopying,
enlarge by 167%

BAG PANEL

straight

grain

place on fold

dalmatian print and
marabou feathers
(pages 68–71)

When photocopying,
enlarge by 200%

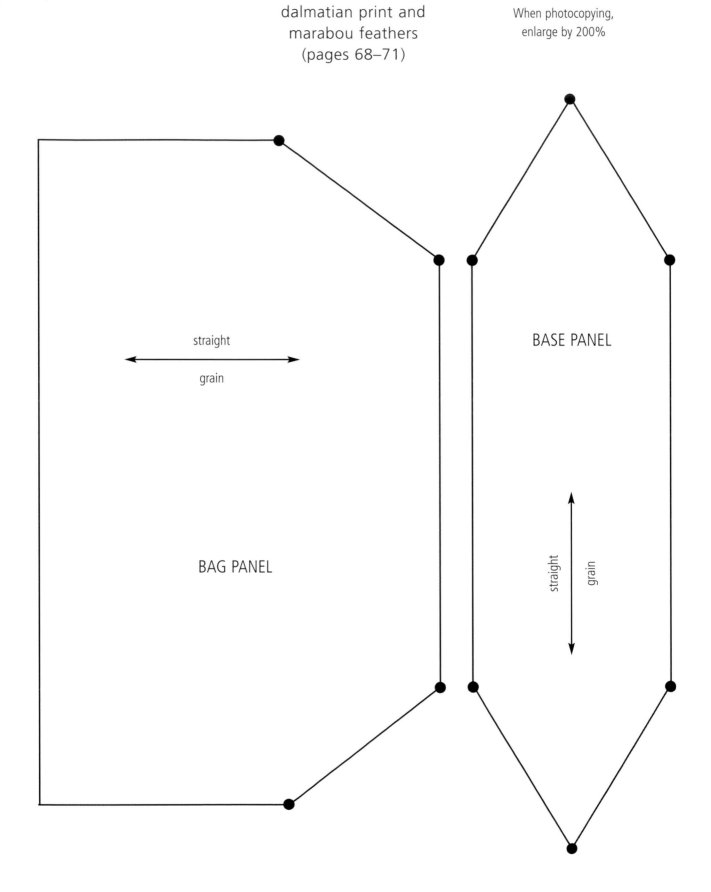

straight

grain

BAG PANEL

BASE PANEL

straight

grain

When photocopying,
enlarge by 200%

gathered tweed handbag
(pages 76–79)

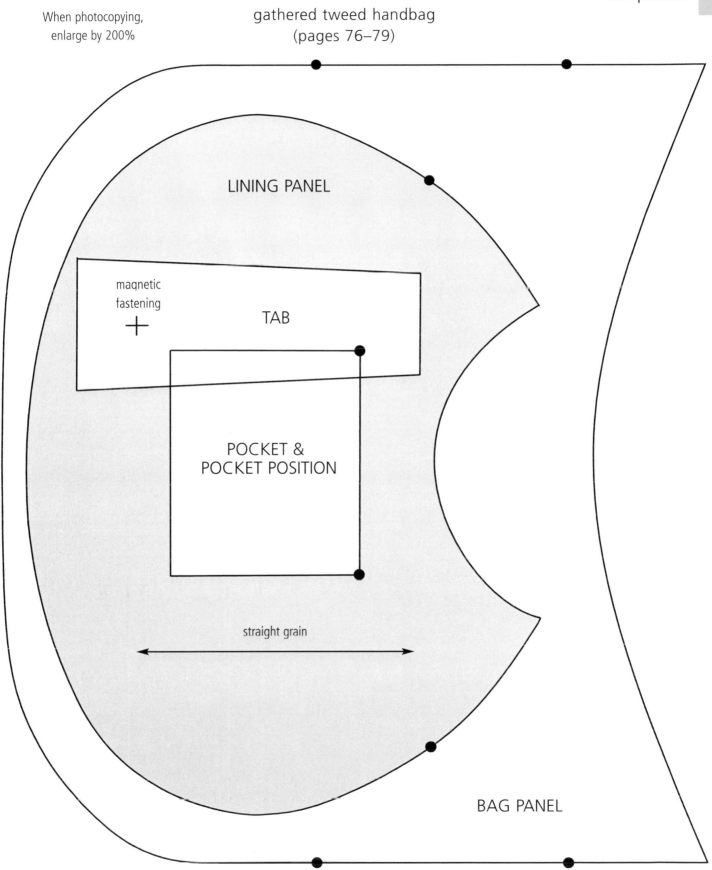

LINING PANEL

magnetic
fastening
+

TAB

POCKET &
POCKET POSITION

straight grain

BAG PANEL

beach bag (pages 78–81)

When photocopying,
enlarge by 167%

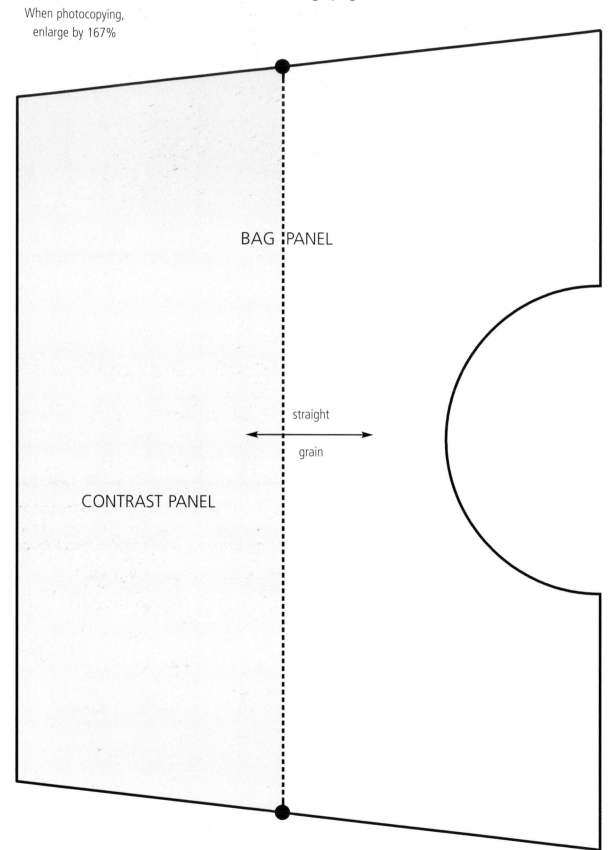

BAG PANEL

straight

grain

CONTRAST PANEL

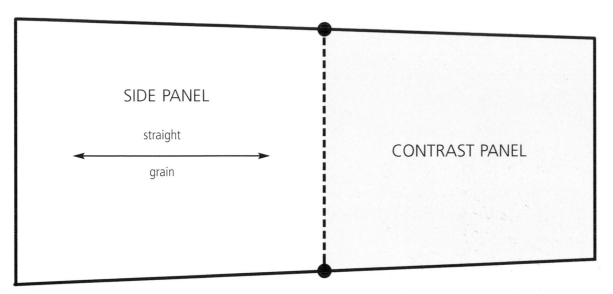

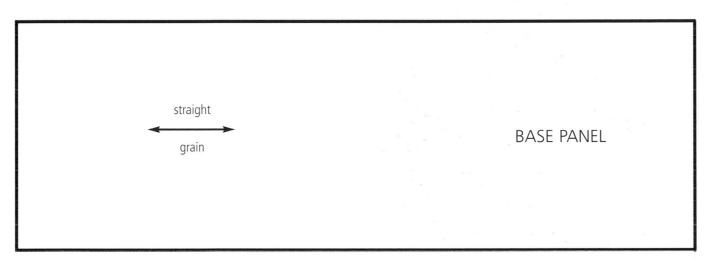

suppliers

UNITED KINGDOM

Bedecked Limited
(*buckles and trimmings*)
Wernwen Farm
Craswall
Hereford HR2 OPP
T: +44 (0)1981 510384
W: www.bedecked.co.uk

Coats Crafts UK
(*bag handles and haberdashery*)
PO Box 22
Lingfield Point
Darlington
Co. Durham DL1 12YQ
T: + 44 (0)1325 394237
W: www.coatscrafts.com

Hobbycraft
(*Pebéo touch, beads, interfacings, haberdashery*)
T: 0800 027 2387 for nearest store
Mail order: +44 (0)1202 596100
W: www.hobbycraft.co.uk

James Hare Silks
(*silk dupion and organza*)
PO Box 72
Monarch House
Queen Street
Leeds LS1 1LX
T: +44 (0)113 243 1204
W: www.jamesharesilks.co.uk

John Lewis Partnership
(*fabrics, interfacings, bag handles, haberdashery, beads*)
Branches nationwide
T: +44 (0)115 941 8282 for nearest store
W: www.johnlewis.com

Kleins
(*acrylic handles, dyes, haberdashery*)
5 Noel Street
London W1F 8GD
T: +44 (0)20 7437 6162
W: www.kleins.co.uk

MacCulloch and Wallis
(*ostrich feather trim, bag handles, fabrics, haberdashery*)
25–26 Dering Street
London W1S 1AT
T: +44 (0)20 7629 0311
E: macculloch@psilink.co.uk

Sinotex UK Ltd
(*ARTY'S readymade undyed bags*)
Unit D, The Courtyard Business Centre
Lonesome Lane, Reigate
Surrey RH2 7QT
T: +44 (0)1737 245450
W: www.artys.co.uk